MW00625492

PASS THE PRAXIS® CORE MATH EXAM

Jerome E. Tuttle

COPYRIGHT 2018

Author	Jerome Tuttle, Lipdom Company, LLC
Publisher	DBC Publishing, Richmond, VA
ISBN	ISBN-13: 978-1-948149-08-2 ISBN-10: 1-948149-08-7
Cover Art	2018© DBC Publishing / Lipdom Company, LLC
Copyright Notice	2018©: All copyrights are reserved. The author supports copyright, which encourages diverse viewpoints, promotes free speech, and creates a vibrant and rich academic culture. Thank you for buying an authorized copy and for complying with international copyright laws. You are supporting the author and other academics to continue to publish. No part of this book, including interior design, cover design, icons, or pictures, may not be reproduced, and/or transmitted in any form, by any means (recording, electronic, photocopying, or otherwise) without the prior written permission of the copyright owner. Independent of the author's economic rights, and even after the transfer of the said rights, the author shall have the right to claim authorship of the work and to object to any distortion, modification of, and/or other derogatory action in relation to the said work that could be deemed prejudicial to the author's honor or reputation. No part of this book or images – black and white, or other renditions of images, are to be posted to any social media, Internet, and/or other digital media or platforms without prior written permission of the copyright owner. The author is waived of any legal or personal responsibility for anything that may happen, regardless of or in despite any direct or related errors or omissions in the content, to the readers taking actions after reading this book.
Trademarks	All brand names, product names, logos, service marks, trademarks or registered trademarks are trademarks of their respective owners.
Author:	You may contact the author with questions, comments, or continuing research inquiries at: fcas80@gmail.com

Table of Contents

Introduction

I cover items in this book after having observed first-hand the math topics students find confusing and having tutored students for the Praxis® exam over the years. More importantly, this book will provide approximately 200 examples and problems for students to practice on that students find confusing.

I wish you good luck on your Praxis® exam!

Jerome E. Tuttle

Jerome E. Tuttle

Chapter 1

Introduction to Praxis
Core Mathematics Exam 5732

Introduction

Do you want to become a teacher? Then you need to pass the Praxis® Core Math or a similar state exam. The Praxis Core Mathematics (5732) exam is given by the Educational Testing Service (ETS). This exam contains 56 short-answer questions you take in a computer-delivered manner in 85 minutes. The exam includes an on-screen, four-function calculator. Topics covered, with brief descriptions:

- Category I: Number and quantity (~ 30%)
- Category II: Algebra and functions (~30%)
- Category III: Geometry (~20%)
- Category IV: Statistics and probability (~20%)

Algebra is the most important topic because you may need it in one of the other categories. Although you do not have to be a math major to take this exam you should have had courses in intermediate (second-year) high school algebra, pre-calculus, or college algebra; and high school or college geometry; you can learn the remaining topics without a course. You should be reviewing topics from a textbook for each of these subjects. If you have taken a course like Math for Elementary Education teachers, the textbook for that course will be helpful. You can self-study probability and statistics if you have never had these courses. You do not need calculus or more advanced math topics required for the middle school or high school Praxis math exams.

You should take advantage of all official materials published by ETS, available at www.ets.org/praxis/prepare/materials/5732

Some states require a similar exam given by Pearson Education, Inc. If your state requires a state-specific exam, you should visit that state's website and take advantage of all official materials published by Pearson Education, Inc. Other than California, these states' exams cover very similar topics to the Praxis 5732 exam.

I teach college math, and I tutor students for this exam. In my opinion, you don't pass math exams by simply memorizing formulas. You pass them by practicing lots of problems. Study guides don't often provide lots of problems or test-taking strategies. In this book, I provide two full-sample exams of problems with suggested solutions and explanations.

Each study-guide author makes his own guess on what topics to cover. We don't know exactly what topics will be on your exam. I have tutored many students for this exam, and I felt most of the study guide problems were easier than what appeared on my students' exams. I deliberately made my problems harder. Some students tell me they believe I get the difficulty of the actual exam 'about right.'

How many problems do you need to get right to pass? No one knows for sure, but I suggest at least 67% and preferably 75%.

Test-Taking Strategies

There are extra test-taking strategies because the Praxis is mostly a multiple-choice exam. These strategies are not necessarily good pedagogy, but you would be foolish to ignore them.

1. Can you plug in the answer choices and see which answer works? If the answer choices are in numerical order, start with a middle answer choice - if that choice doesn't work, hopefully you can figure out whether your next attempt should be higher or lower.
2. Can you use the answer choices to estimate the answer or to look for a factor you may not have considered? For example, if all the answer choices include $\sqrt{3}$, consider what might have to occur in the solution to get to that. If all the answer choices include π, then do your calculations in terms of π.
3. Can you use the more specific results of a general statement to your advantage? For example, if a statement says it is true for all regular polygons, can you use the results of an equilateral triangle? If a statement is true for all integers N, is it true for N=1

and N=2? If a statement is true for all real numbers x, is it true for x=0?

4. The outlier answer choice is probably incorrect. This includes the case where four answer choices include the same item such as √3, but the fifth answer choice does not.

5. Be sure to answer the question asked, not the question you solved or the question you wish they asked. For example, you may have solved a word problem as x = 30 years old, but the question may have asked for the age for not now, but instead for two years ago. Watch out for words like 'always,' 'never,' and 'not.'

6. Try to complete the problem without being influenced by the answer choices. Read all the answer choices - eliminate any choices you are absolutely sure are wrong; do consider one answer may appear right, but another may appear to be even better (more correct). Your first answer choice is usually correct (instinctively), unless you feel you misread the problem.

7. If there are several approaches on a problem, take a moment and then choose the quickest solution. Sometimes trial and error is quickest. Sometimes the online calculator is quickest.

8. If you have not used all the provided information of a problem, you may have overlooked something. Don't make assumptions you can't prove. For example, don't assume an angle is a right angle because it looks like one, don't assume two lines are parallel, etc.

9. As you do a problem, take detailed, clear notes. This will help while you are doing the problem, and if you have time, check your work at the end.

10. If you are doing a calculation with decimals, do not round intermediate calculations; only round to the final answer.

11. If it helps, make a list or draw a diagram. If a diagram is given, feel free to add lines that divide areas.

12. An 85-minute exam with 56 questions averages to about 1.5 minutes per question. With some questions, you may be able to write down the answer in a few seconds, while other questions may be quite time-consuming. Work briskly, but not so fast you become careless. After about 30 minutes (one-third of the total time), check to see whether you have answered about one-third of the questions (19 questions); then decide if you need to work a little quicker, or whether you are working at the right pace.

As you work on a problem think about whether you can do it:

1. in about three minutes or less,
2. whether you can do it, but it will take a lot more time, or
3. whether you don't think you can do it all.

Do the problems you can do in about three minutes or less right away. Make a note of the problems you want to come back to that will take longer, and work on those problems next. Go back and redo the problems you already did (check your work and your detailed notes - look for arithmetic errors like a decimal point or a negative sign). In the last few minutes of the exam, choose any answer choice for the problems you can't do at all; you will at least have a 20% chance of getting the right answer from five choices versus a 100% chance of getting no answer correct.

The Online Four-Function Calculator

A four-function calculator is part of the computer-delivered exam. Below are pointers on how to operate the online calculator.

- You enter an expression such as 3 + 4 * 5 from the computer keyboard, or 3 + 4 x 5 from the calculator keypad, and then press Enter from the computer keyboard or = from the calculator keypad, and the calculator will evaluate the expression using PEMDAS order of operations rules (the answer is 23).
- There is no exponentiation key; if you need to calculate 4^3, then do 4 x 4 x 4 = (the answer).
- You can use parentheses to force an order if you are unsure about the PEMDAS rules.
- The Change Sign button ± changes a positive expression to a negative expression as in 15 ± produces -15.

- To calculate a square root, enter the number and then press the √ key.
- The Transfer Display button will transfer the number displayed on the calculator into the box for numeric entry questions; be careful if the question is asking for a form like a percent or a rounded answer.

Chapter 2: Number and Quantity

Ratios and Proportional Relationships

A ratio is a comparison of two numbers, expressed as a fraction or as two numbers separated by a colon.

Example: 6 boys to 20 children is the ratio 6/20 or 6:20.

A proportion is stating two ratios are equal.

Example: If every class has a ratio of boys to children of 6:20, how many boys are in a class with 30 children?

Answer: Let x = number of boys in the class with 30 children. Solve 6/20 = x/30 and get x = 9.

Note that in a proportion, the numerators must be similar quantities and the denominators must be similar quantities. In the above example, we had 6 boys/20 children = x boys/30 children. If the problem had asked how many girls are in a class with 30 children, it would be incorrect to say 6 boys/20 children = x girls/30 children.

Example: If the ratio of boys to girls is 3:4 and there are 63 students, how many are girls?

Answer: Let x = the proportionality factor, thus 3x + 4x = 63, 7x = 63, x = 9, 4x = 4*9 = 36 girls. Why does this work? This is the equivalent of 3 boys to every 4 girls is 3 boys/4 girls = (3 * 9 boys)/(4 * 9 girls) = 27 boys/36 girls.

Sample Problems:

1. A recipe calls for 2 amounts of ingredient A for each 3 amounts of ingredient B. The amount of ingredient B is 78. How many amounts of ingredient A are there?
2. A set of 60 pens consists of black to blue in the ratio 5:1. How many are black?
3. A class consists of boys, girls, and Martians in a ratio of 20:28:2. There are 168 girls. What is the class total?
4. Ann's cash and Bill's cash were in the ratio 1.3333 to 1. Ann and Bill each spent $15.00. Then their cash was in the ratio 1.5 to 1. How much did they start with?

Solutions to Sample Problems:

1. 2 A's / 3 B's = x A's / 78 B's, x = (2/3)(78) = 52.
2. 5 black/6 total = x black/60 total, x = (5/6)60 = 50.

3. Let x = the proportionality factor, thus 28x = 168, so x = 6. Total = 20x + 28x + 2x = 20 * 6 + 28 * 6 + 2 * 6 = 300.
4. Let x = the proportionality factor. (1.3333x - 15)/(1x - 15) = 1.5/1. Solve for x = 45, which was Bill's starting cash. Ann's starting cash was 1.3333(45) = 60.

The Real Number System

Natural numbers are the counting numbers starting at 1. Zero is not considered a natural number. The whole numbers are the natural numbers plus zero. The integers are positive and negative whole numbers including zero. Negative numbers arise in temperature, in financial loss (a contestant on the TV show Jeopardy may have negative money), and in football yardage.

Rational numbers are numbers expressed as the quotient of two integers. A rational number in decimal form either has a finite number of decimals, or an infinite number of repeating decimals such as .123123123 ... note that an integer is always a rational number. A mixed fraction such as 2½ (2.5) is rational, because it equals 5/2.

An irrational number is a number that cannot be expressed as the quotient of two integers (but proving that is beyond the scope of this exam.) An irrational number has an infinite number of decimals that do not repeat. Square roots of numbers other than perfect squares, such as $\sqrt{2}$, are irrational.

An irrational number can be approximated to whatever number of decimal places by taking one more than that number of decimal places and rounding that final decimal up if it is 5 or greater and down otherwise.

Example: Round the square root of 5 to four decimal places.

Answer: The calculator gives $\sqrt{5}$ as 1.732051. (This itself is rounded.) Five decimal places is 1.73205. The fifth decimal is 5, which rounds up, giving the four-decimal place answer as 1.7321. For a negative number, ignore the negative sign, perform the same steps, then replace the negative sign.

The real numbers are the natural numbers, whole numbers, rational numbers, and irrational numbers. A number like $\sqrt{2}$ is real, even though you cannot hold $\sqrt{2}$ candies in your hand. You can however, walk 1 mile north, 1 mile east, and then exactly $\sqrt{2}$ miles southwest returning where you started.

Within the real number system, you cannot take the square root of a negative number such as $\sqrt{-1}$, because no real number times itself equals -1. There is another number system for such numbers beyond the scope of this course.

A prime number is a natural number that is only divisible by itself and 1, except 1. If a natural number is divisible by something besides itself, then it is composite. The number 1 is neither prime nor composite. Every natural number greater than one can be expressed as a product of prime numbers; this can be useful in calculating the Greatest Common Divisors.

It may be helpful to think of a number line extending infinitely far in both positive and negative directions.

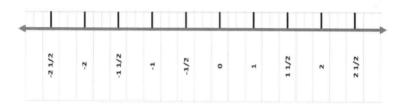

The greater of two numbers is the number to the right of the other on a number line. -1/2 > -2.

Example: Place these numbers in order from smallest to largest: ½, -3/4, -(√2)/2, -7/10.

Answer: If these were all rational numbers you might convert them to a common denominator: 10/20, -15/20, -14/20, and the answer would be - 15/20, -14/20, 10/20; or -3/4, -7/10, .5. But, (√2)/2 is not rational. The better solution is to use the calculator and convert to decimals: .5, -.75, -.707 (rounded), -.7. Then in smallest to largest they are: -.75, -.707, -.7, .5; or -3/4, -(√2)/2, -7/10, .5.

The absolute value of a number may be thought of as how far it is away from zero. We use the symbol "|", as in |6| = 6, and |-6| = 6.

When adding two negative numbers, ignore the negative signs, add the numbers, and make the result negative. When adding a positive number and a negative number, ignore the negative sign, subtract the smaller number from the larger, and then make the result the sign of the larger of the two numbers.

<u>Example</u>: -9 + -4 = -13. -9 + 4 = -5.

When subtracting two numbers, change the sign of the number being subtracted, and then add.

<u>Example</u>: -9 - -4 = -9 + +4 = -5.

A fraction contains a numerator on top, a division bar, and a denominator on bottom. When you enter a fraction in the calculator such as 1/2 =, the result is the decimal equivalent, 0.5. (Note that a calculator only displays a finite number of decimal places.) A proper fraction is less than 1 if it is positive such as 2/3, or it is greater than -1 if it is negative such as -2/3. An improper fraction has its numerator greater than its denominator, ignoring any negative signs), such as 7/4.

A mixed number contains a whole number and a proper fraction such as 1 ¾. To change a mixed number into an improper fraction, multiply the

$$\frac{13}{4}$$

4·1 13
———
4   4 ... 7/4

denominator by the whole number, add the numerator, and divide the result by the denominator.

Example: Change 1¾ to an improper fraction.

Answer: 1¾ = (4 x 1 + 3)/4 = ⁷/₄.

✳ Note that a negative mixed number such as -1¾ equals -(1¾). It does **not** equal -1+¾, which equals - 1/4.

The Least Common Multiple (LCM) is the smallest multiple of two or more whole numbers. (Here, "least common" means smallest common; it does not mean most uncommon!)

Example: The multiples of 3 are 3, 6, 9, 12, 15, 18, 21, 24, etc. The multiples of 4 are 4, 8, 12, 16, 20, 24, etc.; 24 is a common multiple of both 3 and 4, but it is not the least common multiple. Twelve is the least common multiple. The LCM is used adding or subtracting fractions having different denominators.

The Greatest Common Divisor (GCD) is the largest number that divides two or more whole numbers.

Example: The divisors of 8 are 1, 2, 4, 8. The divisors of 12 are 1, 2, 3, 4, 6, 12; 4 is the greatest common divisor of 8 and 12. This is used in reducing fractions to lowest terms: $8/_{12} = (2*4)/(3*4) = 2/_3$. GCD's can be computed by determining prime factorizations of the two numbers.

To add or subtract fractions having the same denominator, add or subtract the numerators and retain the denominator. To add or subtract fractions having different denominators, first choose a common denominator that is a multiple of both fractions (preferably, but not necessarily the least common denominator), convert each fraction to an equivalent fraction having that common denominator, then add or subtract these new numerators and retain the common denominator.

To multiply fractions, multiply the numerators and then multiply the denominators. To divide fractions, flip the second fraction, and then multiply the result. Never divide by 0; this is not a permissible calculation.

Example: Add $1/_3 + 3/_4$. 12 is the least common multiple. Multiply the first fraction by $4/_4$ (you may always multiply a number by 1 without changing the result) and multiply the second fraction by $3/_3$: $(1/_3)$ $(4/_4) + (3/_4)(3/_3) = (1x4)/(3x4) + (3x3)/(4x3) = 4/_{12} + 9/_{12}$ $= 13/_{12} = 11/_{12}$.

An exponent is used for repeated multiplication. The problem 3 x 3 x 3 x 3 which equals 81 is written 3^4, where 4 is called the exponent and 3 is called the base. In multiplying two numbers with the same base, the exponents add:

$3^2 \times 3^4 = 3^{2+4} = 3^6 = 729$.

In dividing two numbers with the same base, the exponents subtract: $3^6 / 3^4 = 3^{6-4} = 3^2 = 9$. A negative exponent is the reciprocal of its positive exponent: $3^{-4} = 1 / 3^4 = 1/81$. In raising an expression with an exponent to another exponent, the exponents multiply: $(3^2)^4 = 3^{2 \times 4} = 3^8 = 6{,}561$. In a fractional exponent, the denominator indicates the root (as in square root or cube root): $9^{1/2} = \sqrt{9} = 3$. Any non-zero base with a 0 exponent equals 1, such as $2^0 = 1$.

The square root of a number is a value that – when multiplied by itself – gives the original number. The square root of 9 is 3 because $3 \times 3 = 9$; we write this as $\sqrt{9} = \sqrt{(3 \times 3)} = 3$, and we also write this as $9^{1/2} = 3$. It is true that $(-3 \times -3) = 9$, but when we use the $\sqrt{}$ symbol, we mean the positive square root. If we wanted both the positive and negative square roots, we would write $\pm\sqrt{}$, as in $\pm\sqrt{9}$ equals +3 and -3. The perfect squares are $1^2 = 1$, $2^2 = 4$, $3^2 = 9$, $4^2 = 16$, $5^2 = 25$, etc., and the square roots of perfect squares are whole numbers. Square roots of counting numbers that are perfect squares will be rational numbers, while square roots of counting numbers that are not perfect squares will be irrational numbers. For any positive numbers x and y, $\sqrt{(xy)} = \sqrt{x} * \sqrt{y}$. Square root and absolute value are related by $\sqrt{(x^2)} = |x|$.

In scientific notation, a number is written as a decimal whose absolute value is between 1 and 10, times a power of 10, such as $123456 = 1.23456 \times 10^5$, and $-.00123456 = -1.23456 \times 10^{-3}$.

A percent is a ratio of a number divided by 100.

90% = $^{90}/_{100}$ = .90. There are three common percent problems; they are variations of "A is P percent of B". You are given two of A, P, and B, and you solve for the unknown one. Change the percent to a decimal. Note that 'of' generally means multiply and 'is' generally means equal.

Example: What is 90% of 300?

Answer: .90 x 300 = 270.

Example: 270 is 90% of what number?

Answer: Let the number be x. .90(x) = 270, x = 270/.9 = 300.

Example: 270 is what percent of 300?

Answer: 270/300 = .90 = 90%.

A percent change is the amount of change divided by the old amount; the amount of the change may be positive or negative. The new amount equals the old amount plus the amount of the change. If you are given the new and old amounts, then the percent change equals (new/old - 1) x 100%.

Example: The original price was $300, but it is on sale for $270. What is the percent discount?

Answer: Use (new/old - 1) x 100% = ($^{270}/_{300}$ - 1) x 100% = (.90 - 1) x 100% = -.10 x 100% = -10%.

Quantities

A unit fraction has a numerator and denominator with different units, and the value of the fraction is one. In converting from one unit of measurement to another, multiply the value in the old units by a unit fraction equal to the quotient of new units divided by old units, so the old units cancel.

You should know millimeter, centimeter, meter, and kilometer conversions.

Example: If 1 British pound £ equals $1.31 US dollars, then $100 equals $100 x (1 £ / $1.31) = 76.34£.

Problems:

1. Is $(\sqrt{7})/2$ rational or irrational?

2. 22/7 is an approximation of π. Is this approximation rational or irrational?

3. Find a number between $-\pi/3$ and $-\pi/2$ and leave the answer in terms of π.

4. Is 23 a prime number? If not, find all its factors other than itself and 1.

5. Is 51 a prime number? If not, find all its factors other than itself and 1.

6. Place these numbers in order from smallest to largest; round final answers to three decimal places: $-\pi/2$, $-\sqrt{(\pi/2)}$, $-\sqrt{(\pi)}/2$, $-(\sqrt{(\pi/2)})^{1/2}$, $-(\sqrt{(\pi/2)})^{-1/2}$

7. Add these numbers: a. -10 + -3. b. -3 + 8. c. 9

   -13   *5*

   + -13. d. -8.1 + 1.5. e. -6.5 + - 4.8.

   -4   *-6.6*   *-11.3*

8. Subtract these numbers: a. -10 - (-3). b. -3 - 8.

   -7   *-11*

   c. 9 - (-13). d. -8.1 - 1.5. e. -6.5 - (-4.8). f.

   22   *-9.6*   *1.7*

   -3 -(x-1).

   -2 -x

9. Change these mixed numbers into improper

   fractions: a. $2\frac{5}{8}$. b. $4\frac{1}{2}$. c. $-4\frac{5}{6}$. d. $-3\frac{2}{9}$.

10. Change these improper fractions into mixed

    numbers: a. $^{11}/_5$. b. $^{-37}/_5$. c. $^{72}/_{16}$.

11. Add these fractions: a. $^2/_5 + ^4/_9$. b. $^1/_5 + ^2/_3$.

    c. $^3/_5 + -^3/_8$. d. $^3/_4 + ^3/_{11}$.

12. Suppose Ann jogs 3 laps per hour, Bill jogs 4 laps

    per hour, and they start together. After how

    many laps will they be at the starting point at

    the same time?

13. Suppose I eat fish every 6 days, drink milk every 4 days, and have desert every 16 days, and suppose I ate all of these today. When is the next time I will eat all 3 on the same day?

14. Calculate: a. $4^{3/2}$. b. $(3^4)^{-1/2}$.

15. Write in scientific notation: a. 9876.54321. b. - .0123123

16. 12 is 15% of what number? 80

17. 25 is what percent of 62.5?

18. What is 55% of 300?

19. A $150 item is reduced in price by 25%, and then that price is reduced by 10%. What is the final price?

20. A rectangular rug is 10 feet by 12 feet. How big is the area in square yards?

21. Ann has $140 in a bank account that pays no interest. She adds a constant dollar amount each month, and 4 months later she has $200 in the account. If she continues adding the same constant dollar amount, how much will she have 9 months after she began?

22. What is the greatest common divisor of 56 and 98?

23. Calculate $\sqrt{320} - \sqrt{192}$; but leave the answer in terms of square roots.

24. Let S be the statement, "All quadrilaterals having four equal sides are squares." Either agree that the statement is always true or provide a counterexample.

25. Suppose a class election produced the following results. How many candidates got at least 22% of the votes?

	Votes
Candidate A	12	*1*
Candidate B	15
Candidate C	18
Candidate D	3
Candidate E	12	*2*

60

60 X 0.22 = 13.2

Solutions to Problems:

1. Seven is not a perfect square, so $\sqrt{7}$ is irrational. Since it is irrational, it is not an integer. So $(\sqrt{7})/2$ is irrational.

2. The fraction, $^{22}/_7$, is the quotient of two integers, so this is rational.

3. Use a common denominator of 6, and then take an average: $-\pi/3 = -2\pi/6$, and $-\pi/2 = -3\pi/6$. $(-2\pi/6 + -3\pi/6)/2 = (-5\pi/6)/2 = -5\pi/12$.

4. The number 23 is prime; its only divisors are itself and 1.

5. The number 51 is not prime; its divisors are 3 and 17.

6. Use the calculator, and approximate π as 3.14. -

   $\pi/2 \approx -1.570$; $-\sqrt{(\pi/2)} \approx -1.253$; $-\sqrt{(\pi)}/2 \approx -.886$, -

   $(\sqrt{(\pi/2)})^{1/2} \approx -1.119$; $-(\sqrt{(\pi/2)})^{-1/2} \approx -.893$.

   Answer: $-\pi/2$, $-\sqrt{(\pi/2)}$, $-(\sqrt{(\pi/2)})^{1/2}$, $-(\sqrt{(\pi/2)})^{-1/2}$, -

   $\sqrt{(\pi)}/2$.

7. a. -10 + -3 = -13. b. -3 + 8 = +5. c. 9 + -13 = -

   4. d. -8.1 + 1.5 = -6.6. e. -6.5 + - 4.8 = -1.7.

8. When subtracting two numbers, change the sign of

   the number being subtracted, and then add.

   a. -10 - -3 = -10 + (+3) = -7. b. -3 - 8 = -3 + (-

   8) = -11. c. 9 - (-13) = 9 + (+13) = +22. d. -

   8.1 - 1.5 = -8.1 + (-1.5) = -9.6. e. -6.5 - (-4.8)

   = -6.5 + (+4.8) = -2.3. f. -3 -(x - 1) = -3 + -(x-1)

   = -3 - x + 1 = -2 - x.

9. a. $2\dfrac{5}{8} = (8 \times 2 + 5)/8 = {}^{21}/_8$. b. $3\dfrac{4}{7} = (7 \times 3 + 4)/7$

   $= {}^{25}/_7$. c. $-4\dfrac{5}{6} = -(6 \times 4 + 5)/6 = {}^{-29}/_6$. d. $-3\dfrac{2}{9} =$

   $-(9 \times 3 + 2)/9 = {}^{-29}/_9$.

10. a. $^{11}/_5$ = 2 with a remainder of 1, or $2\dfrac{1}{5}$.

b. $^{-37}/_5$ = -7 with a remainder of 2, or $-7\dfrac{2}{5}$.

c. $^{72}/_{16}$ = 4 with a remainder of 8, or $4\dfrac{8}{16}$

or $4\dfrac{1}{2}$.

11. a. The Least Common Multiple (LCM) of 5 and 9

is 45, (2/5)(9/9) + (4/9)(5/5) = 18/45 + 20/45 =

38/45. b. 1/5 + 2/3 = (1/5)(3/3) + (2/3)(5/5) =

3/15 + 10/15 = 13/15. c. 3/5 + (-3/8) =

(3/5)(8/8) + - (3/8)(5/5) = 24/40 - 15/40 = 9/40.

d. 3/4 + 3/11 = (3/4)(11/11) + (3/11)(4/4) =

33/44 + 12/44 = 55/44. ? 45/44

12. This problem equivalently asks for the least

common multiple of 3 and 4, which is 12.

13. This problem equivalently asks for the least

common multiple of 6, 4 and 16, which is 48.

14. a. $4^{3/2} = \sqrt{(4^3)} = \sqrt{(64)} = 8$. b. $(3^4)^{-1/2} = 3^{(4*-1/2)} =$

$3^{-2} = 1/3^2 = 1/9$.

15. a. 9876.54321: to move decimal point three to

the left, divide by 1,000 and multiply by 1,000.

$(9876.54321/1,000) * 1,000 = 9.87654321 \times 10^3$.

b. -.0123123: to move decimal point two to the

right, multiply by 100 and divide by 100.

$(-.0123123 \times 100) / 100 = -1.23123 \times 10^{-2}$.

16. 12 is 15% of what number? Let the number be x.

$.15(x) = 12$, $x = 12/.15 = 80$.

17. The number 25 is what percent of 62.5? $^{25}/_{62.5} =$

$.40 = 40\%$.

18. What is 55% of 300? $.55 \times 300 = 165$.

19. The first amount of change is $150.00 \times .25 =$

37.5, so the first new price is $150.00 - 37.5 =$

$112.50. The second amount of change is

$112.50 \times .10 = 11.25, so the final new price

is $112.50 - 11.25 = $101.25.

20. 10 feet by 12 feet equals 120 square feet; 3 feet = 1 yard; (3 feet)^2 = (1 yard)^2; 9 square feet = 1 square yard; (120 square feet) x (1 square yard / 9 square feet) = 13.33 square yards.

21. Each month she adds (200 - 140)/4 = 15. In 9 months, she will have 140 + 9 * 15 = 275.

22. 56 = 7 * 2 * 2 * 2, and 98 = 7 * 7 * 2. Each of these has 7 * 2 = 14 in common; 14 is the GCD.

23. $\sqrt{320}$ - $\sqrt{192}$ = $\sqrt{(64 \times 5)}$ - $\sqrt{(64 \times 3)}$ = $\sqrt{64}\sqrt{5}$ - $\sqrt{64}\sqrt{3}$ = $8\sqrt{5}$ - $8\sqrt{3}$ = $8(\sqrt{5} - \sqrt{3})$.

24. A counterexample to "All quadrilaterals having four equal sides are squares" is "A rhombus is a quadrilateral having four equal sides that is not a square."

25. Convert to percentages; answer: 2.

	Votes	Percent	≥ 22%
Candidate A	12	20%	
Candidate B	15	25%	Yes

	Votes	Percent	≥ 22%
Candidate C	18	30%	Yes
Candidate D	3	5%	
Candidate E	12	20%	
Total	60	100%	

Chapter 3: Algebra and Functions

Why do I have to study algebra? I'll never use it. Here is a real problem brought to my attention: Gregory was a history major in college, and through his junior year he had taken eight, 3-credit history courses with a GPA of 2.5. However, his college requires a history GPA of at least 3.0 to graduate with a history degree. How many additional 3-credit history courses does he need to pass with a 4.0 so his total history GPA will be at least a 3.0? Gregory met with his advisor, the chairperson, and the dean, and none of them recognized this as an algebra problem that could be solved as
$(8 * 2.5 + x * 4)/(8 + x) = 3$; the answer is $x = 4$.

Algebra, pronounced al'-juh-bruh, is a branch of mathematics that substitutes letters for numbers to express relationships. The word 'algebra' is derived from an Arabic word dated to around the year 830, but the word's origins go back to around the year 1600 BCE from the ancient Babylonians. Ancient civilizations in Egypt, China, and the Islamic Arab Empire are among those that contributed to the development of algebra. The symbol x, as an unknown variable, is attributed to Descartes in 1637.

Basic Concepts

A variable is a letter that represents numbers; the numbers may change. A constant is a number that does not change. A term is a product or quotient of constants and variables such as $3x^2$, or $3x^2/7y^4$. An expression is the combination of terms. The constant part of the term is called the coefficient. Like terms are terms which differ only in their coefficients, like $-3x^2y^4$ and $5x^2y^4$; the importance of like terms is that like terms are added or subtracted using their coefficients: $-3x^2y^4 + 5x^2y^4 = 2x^2y^4$.

The degree of a term such as $4x^3y^2z$ equals the sum of the exponents of the variables: $3 + 2 + 1 = 6$. A polynomial is the sum of terms whose exponents of its variables are all positive counting numbers. The degree of a polynomial is the degree of the highest term; for example, the polynomial $1 - 3x + 4x^2$ has a degree of 2.

When an expression is contained inside parentheses, and a negative sign precedes the parentheses, you may remove the parentheses, but you must change the sign of each term. For example, $-(-3x^2y^4 + 5x^3y^2) = +3x^2y^4 - 5x^3y^2$. Note these are not like terms, so they cannot be further combined.

An equation is a statement of equality between two expressions. An equation may be true for only certain values of unknown variables, such as $x + 1 = 3$ is only true for $x = 2$, or an equation may be true for all permissible values of the unknown variables, such as $(x^2 - 1) = (x + 1)(x - 1)$.

In solving an equation with a single unknown variable x, the goal is to transform the equation to get x alone on one side of the ('equal sign') equation. The following operations are permitted: A number may be added, or subtracted, or multiplied, or divided to both sides of the equation and the equation is still valid. Both sides of an equation may be raised to the same power (if x = 3, then x^2 = 3^2 = 9), but when raising to an even power this introduces the possibility of an extra solution (here, x = -3) that may not satisfy the original equation.

The operations of addition, subtraction, multiplication, and division may also be applied to both sides of an inequality, but there is an additional rule for inequalities: when multiplying or dividing both sides of an inequality by a negative number, the direction of the inequality is changed.

Example: If -x < -3, then (-1)(-x) >(-1)(-3), and x>3. In interval notation, x>3 becomes (3,∞); if instead we wanted x≥3, its interval notation is [3,∞).

How to Solve a Linear Equation Having a Single Unknown Variable

A linear equation has a variable such as x that does not have an exponent other than 1. The goal is to transform the equation to get x alone on one side of the equation.

Example: Solve for x: $3x - 7 = 5$.

Answer: We want to get x alone on the left side. Get rid of the 7 on the left by adding 7 to both sides of the equation:

$$3x - 7 + 7 = 5 + 7, 3x = 12, x = 4$$

Note that although an alternative first step might have been to divide both sides by 3, that would give $(3x - 7)/3 = 5/3, 3x/3 - 7/3 = 5/3, x - 7/3 = 5/3$, we would still have to get rid of the 7, which has become 7/3, and we have not made this easier or saved any time.

Example: Solve for x: $5(x + 2) = 3(x - 4)$.

Answer: Use the distributive property to remove parentheses.

$$5x + 10 = 3x - 12$$

Get rid of the 10 on the left by subtracting 10 from both sides of the equation; $5x + 10 - 10 = 3x - 12 - 10, 5x = 3x - 22$. Get rid of the 3x on the right by subtracting 3x from both sides; $5x - 3x = 3x - 22 - 3x$, $2x = -22$. Get rid of the 2 on the right by dividing both sides of the equation by 2. $2x/2 = -22/2, x = -11$.

Example: Solve for x: (9 - x)/(x - 3) = 2.

Answer: Get rid of the (x - 3) in the denominator by multiplying both sides of the equation by (x - 3): ((9 - x)/(x - 3))(x - 3) = 2(x - 3), 9 - x = 2(x - 3) = 2x - 6. Get rid of the -x on the left by adding x to both sides; 9 - x + x = 2x - 6 + x, 9 = 3x - 6. Get rid of the -6 on the right by adding 6 to both sides; 9 + 6 = 3x - 6 + 6, 15 = 3x. Get rid of the 3 on the right by dividing both sides by 3. 15/3 = 3x/3, 5 = x, or x = 5.

Example: Solve for x: -2(x + 3) < 12.

Answer: Use the distributive property to remove parentheses. -2x -6 < 12. Get rid of the -6 on the left by adding 6 to both sides. -2x -6 + 6 < 12 + 6, -2x < 18. Get rid of the -2 on the left by dividing both sides by -2 but change the direction of the inequality. -2x/-2 > 18/-2, x > -9. Note for example that -7, which is greater than -9, satisfies the original inequality: -2(-7 + 3) = -2 * -4 = 8 < 12; but -11, which is less than -9, does not: -2(-11 + 3) = -2 * -8 = 16 > 12.

Example: Solve for x: |x - 5|<3.

Answer: This is equivalent to -3 < x - 5 < +3. Add + 5 to all three terms, so 2 < x < 8. The solution interval is (2,8).

<u>Example</u>: Solve for x: $|x - 5| > 3$.

<u>Answer</u>: This is equivalent to two inequalities: $x - 5 > 3$, and $x - 5 < -3$. Add $+ 5$ to all four terms, so $x > 8$, or $x < 2$. The solution interval is $(-\infty, 2) \cup (8, \infty)$.

Functions

A function is a set of ordered pairs, so each first member of an ordered pair is matched with only one second member. With ordered pairs, the first member is usually called the x value, and the second value is usually called the y value. The set $A = \{(1,1), (2,1)\}$ is a function, while the set $B \{(1,1), (1,-1)\}$ is not a function. The set of first members is called the domain, and the set of second members is called the range. A function may be expressed in set notation, as a table of values, or as an equation. In equation notation, the function may have a letter, often f, g, or h, as in $f(x) = x^2$. Not every set of ordered pairs, table, or equation is a function; for example $y^2 = x$ which includes ordered pairs $(1,1)$, $(1,-1)$ is not a function.

Ordered pairs may be drawn (graphed) on an xy coordinate system, where the horizontal axis is called the x-axis, and the vertical axis is called the y-axis. The intersection of the x and y-axes is called the origin, or $(0,0)$ point. The following chart shows the graph of a point $(-3,2)$, which is three units to the left of the origin and two units above the origin.

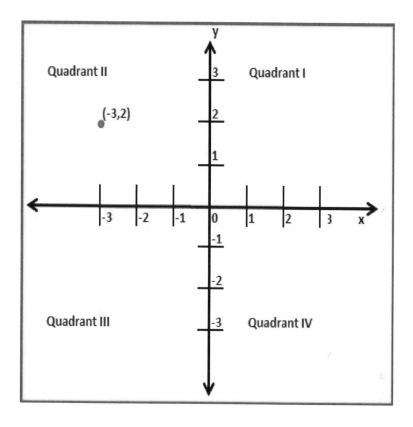

An equation may be drawn on an xy coordinate system by graphing points. The vertical line test is a visual way to determine if the graph of a curve is a function or not. If every vertical line intersects the curve at no more than one value, then the curve is a function. If a vertical line intersects the curve at two or more values, then the curve is not a function. $y = x^2$ is a function, but $x = y^2$ is not a function.

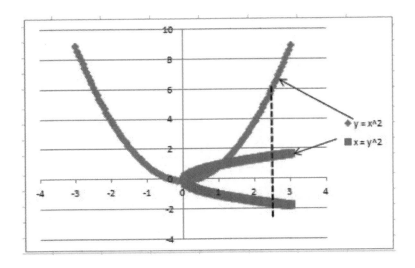

The equation $y = x^2$ is called a quadratic equation because of the x^2 term. A quadratic equation is U-shaped, although the U may be upside-down or sideways. Looking at the graph of $y = x^2$ above, you will note that as you read the graph from left to right, as x increases from negative infinity towards zero, the y values of the curve decrease; and as x increases from zero toward positive infinity, the y values of the curve increase. Looking at the graph of $x = y^2$ above, you will note the upper branch only has increasing values of y, while the lower branch only has decreasing values of y.

Linear Equations and Graphs

A linear equation in x and y such as $3x + 4y = 12$ has its two variables having exponents equal to 1. The graph of a linear equation is always a straight line. The slope of a line describes its steepness and its direction. The slope is denoted m and is defined as the ratio of vertical change divided by horizontal change or change in y divided by change in x: $\Delta y/\Delta x$. If (x_1, y_1) and (x_2, y_2) are any two points on the line, then $m = (y_2 - y_1)/(x_2 - x_1)$. The slope of a straight line is the same regardless of which the points you choose. If $m > 0$, the slope is positive, and the line is increasing. If $m < 0$, the slope is negative, and the line is decreasing. If $m = 0$, the slope is zero and the line is horizontal. If the line is vertical (because $x_2 = x_1$ and the denominator of $m = 0$), then the slope is undefined.

If two lines intersect, then the point of intersection is the solution to both equations simultaneously. If two lines are parallel, they have equal slopes, and there is no solution to both equations simultaneously. If two lines are perpendicular (intersect at a right angle), then the product of their slopes is -1 (as long as neither line is vertical).

Example: Find the slope of the straight line passing through the points (-3,-1) and (-2,4).

Answer: Let $(x_1, y_1) = (-3,1)$ and $(x_2, y_2) = (-2,4)$. Then $m = (y_2 - y_1)/(x_2 - x_1) = (4 - (-1))/(-2- (-3)) = 5/1 = 5$.

The y-intercept of a line is denoted by b and is the y value where the line intersects the x-axis (where $x = 0$). If you know the slope m and the y-intercept b, then the equation of its straight line is $y = mx + b$.

Equivalently, if you know the slope m and any one point (x_1, y_1) on the line, then the equation of its straight line is $y - y_1 = m(x - x_1)$. If you are given an equation of a straight line and you are asked to graph that line, choose any two points on the line (such as choose $x = 0$, plug it into the equation and find its y value; then repeat with $x = 1$), draw those points on an xy coordinate system, connect the points with a straight line, and continue the line in both directions.

Example: Find the slope and y-intercept of the line $4x + 3y = 4$.

Answer: First put it in the form of $y = mx + b$: $4x + 3y = 4$, $3y = -4x + 4$, $y = (-4/3)x + 4/3$. The slope is -4/3, and the y-intercept is 4/3.

Example: Find the equation of the straight line passing through points (-2.9,5.2) and (-2,4).

Answer: Calculate $m = (4 - 5.2)/(-2 - (-2.9)) = -1.2/.9 = -4/3$. Choose (-2,4), and plug into $y - y_1 = m(x - x_1)$: $y - 4 = (-4/3)(x - (-2))$, $y - 4 = (-4/3)(x + 2)$, $y = (-4/3)(x + 2) + 4 = (-4/3)x + 4/3$.

Problems:

1. Add: $(5x^4y + 7x^3y^2 - 10x^2y^3 - 11) + (-5x^3y^2 - 2x^4y + 3xy^4 + 8)$.

2. What is the value of the expression $8 - (7-5)^2 + 10/5 * 4$?

3. Simplify this expression: $x(x^2 - 2y) - x^2(x + 2y)$.

4. Simplify this expression: $\dfrac{\frac{1}{x} - 1}{\frac{2}{x}}$

5. If $2(3x + 1) = 14$, what is the value of $-x^2 + 5$?

6. Solve for x: $16 - x/5 = 10$.

7. Solve for x: $-7x + 4 = -25x + 1$.

8. Solve for x: $-3x + 7 \geq 13$. Plot the solution on a number line.

9. If $f(x) = x^3 - 2x^2$, calculate $f(3) - f(2)$.

10. Let S = {(George, Washington), (John, Adams), (Tom, Jefferson), (Andrew, Johnson), (Lyndon, Johnson)}. Is this a function? Why or why not?

11. Let $f(x) = (x^2 + 5)/\sqrt{(5 - 3x)}$.   What is the domain of f?

12. Let $f(x) = \sqrt{(16 - x)} + 1/(x-2)$. What is the domain of f?

13. What are the slope, y-intercept, and x-intercept of the line $12x - 3y = 24$?

14. Write the equation of the line that is parallel to $y = 2x - 5$ and contains the point (1,1); then draw your equation on a xy coordinate system.

15. Draw the solution to $2x - y \geq 1$ on an xy coordinate system. Identify one point that satisfies the inequality, and another point that does not.

16. Draw the graphs of 2x - y = 4 and x + y = 5. Then find their simultaneous solution graphically.

17. Use the graph below of y = x⁴ - 8x² to identify on which intervals y is increasing or decreasing.

y=x^4 - 8x^2

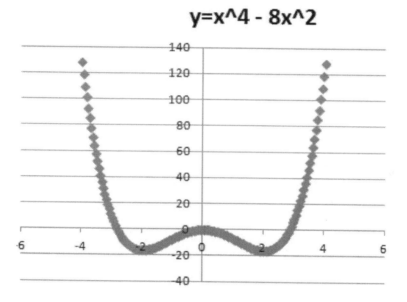

18. Consider the following data on city population (in table below): Would you say the best function to describe this data is a straight line, a parabola, or an exponential function?

Year	2014	2015	2016	2017	2018
Population	100,000	105,000	110,250	115,763	121,551

19. Solve the equation $\sqrt{x - 3} = +1$.

20. Solve the equation $\sqrt{x - 3} = -1$.

Solutions to Problems:

1. Rewrite vertically instead of horizontally, and

   rearrange terms:

   $5x^4y + 7x^3y^2 - 10x^2y^3$ $\qquad$ $- 11$

   $-2x^4y - 5x^3y^2$ $\qquad$ $+ 3xy^4 + 8$

   $3x^4y + 2x^3y^2 - 10x^2y^3$ $\quad$ $+ 3xy^4 - 3$

2. $8 - (7-5)^2 + 10/5*4 = 8 - (2)^2 + 2*4 = 8 - 4 + 8 = 12$.

3. $3x(x^2 - 2y) - 2x^2(x + 2y) = (3x^3 - 6xy) + (-2x^3 - 4x^2y)$

   $= x^3 - 4x^2y - 6xy$.

4. $(1/x - 1)/(2/x) = (1/x - 1)*(x/2) = ((1 - x)/x)*(x/2)$

   $= (1 - x)/2$.

5. $2(3x + 1) = 14$, $6x + 2 = 14$, $6x = 12$, $x = 2$. $-2^2 + 5$

   $= -(2^2) + 5 = - 4 + 5 = +1$.

6. $16 - x/5 = 10$, $16 - 10 = x/5$, $6 = x/5$, $x = 30$.

7. $-7x + 4 = -25x + 1$, $18x = -3$, $x = -3/18 = -1/6$.

8. $-3x + 7 \geq 13$, $-3x \geq 6$, divide by -3 and change the direction of the inequality, $x \leq -2$. The number line looks as follows. Note at -2 there is a filled-in circle indicating -2 is part of the solution. If the solution had been $x < -2$, then the circle would not be filled in.

9. $f(x) = x^3 - 2x^2$, $f(3) = 3^3 - 2 * 3^2 = 27 - 2 * 9 = 9$;

$f(2) = 2^3 - 2 * 2^2 = 2^3 - 2^3 = 0$. Answer: 9.

10. This is a set of ordered pairs. They do not have to be numbers. Does each first member of an ordered pair match with only one second member? Yes. This is a function.

11. The set of first members of the ordered pairs of a function is called the domain.

$f(x) = (x^2 + 5)/\sqrt{(5 - 3x)}$; are there any values of x that cannot be part of this function? In the numerator, all values are possible. In the denominator, the square root cannot be negative. We need $5 - 3x \geq 0$, $5 \geq 3x$, $5/3 \geq x$, or $x \leq 5/3$.

12. $f(x) = \sqrt{(16 - x)} + 1/(x-2)$. In the first term, the square root cannot be negative. We need $16 - x \geq 0$, $x \leq 16$. In the second term, the denominator cannot be 0, which occurs at x=2. The answer is $x \leq 16$, excluding $x = 2$.

13. $12x - 3y = 24$. Rearrange into $y = mx + b$ form: $-3y = -12x + 24$, $y = 4x - 8$. $m = 4$, $b = -8$. The y-intercept b is the value of y when $x = 0$. The x-intercept is the value of x when $y = 0$: $y = 4x - 8$, $0 = 4x - 8$, $x = 2$.

14. A line parallel to y = 2x - 5 will have the same

slope, 2. Using $y - y_1 = m(x - x_1)$, and

containing the point (1,1), we have

y - 1 = 2(x - 1), or y = 2x - 2 + 1, or y = 2x - 1.

Note the graph of y = 2x -1 has slope 2 and

y-intercept -1.

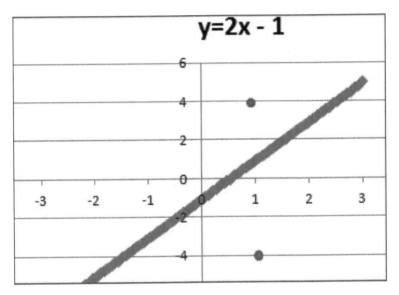

15. 2x - y ≥ 1, 2x - 1 ≥ y, y ≤ 2x - 1. The solution set

is the line y = 2x - 1 and the area below the

line. (The line is part of the solution because of

the equality part of the ≤ symbol.) (1,-4) is one

point that is part of the solution set and -4 is

less than or equal 2 * 1 - 1; (1,4) is one point

that is not part of the solution set, and 4 is

greater than 2*1 - 1.

16. 2x - y = 4 and x + y = 5 are equivalent to

y = 2x - 4 and y = -x + 5. Their graphs

intersect at (3,2).

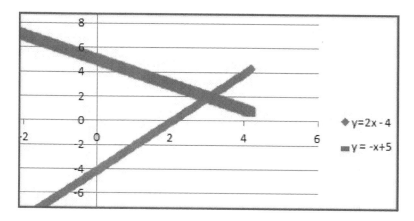

17. y is decreasing for -∞ < x < -2 and 0 < x < 2; and

increasing for -2 < x < 0 and 2 < x < ∞.

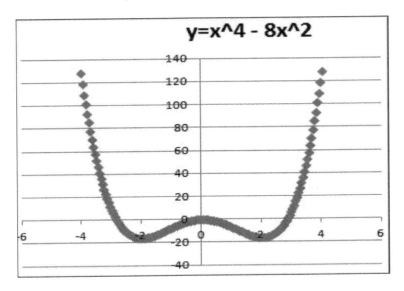

18. If this were a straight line, the annual increase

would be an equal amount such as 5,000 per

year. It is not U-shaped. It is actually

increasing 5% per year, which is exponential.

Year	2014	2015	2016	2017	2018
Population	100,000	105,000	110,250	115,763	121,551

19. Solve the equation $\sqrt{(x - 3)} = +1$ by squaring both

sides. $(\sqrt{(x - 3)})^2 = (+1)^2$, $x - 3 = 1$, $x = 4$.

20. Solve the equation $\sqrt{(x-3)} = -1$ by squaring both sides. $\sqrt{(x-3)} = -1$, $(\sqrt{(x-3)})^2 = (-1)^2$, $x - 3 = 1$, $x = 4$. This extraneous solution does not solve the original equation. There is no solution.

Word Problems

With word problems, you are given some text, and you need to translate the text into algebraic expressions and equations. Read the problem carefully. Assign a variable name to the variable you know least about and try to express the other variables in terms of that first variable.

Put your information into an equation. Solve the equation. Then answer the problem. For this exam, there will probably not be any unnecessary given information, so if you have not used all the given information, then you are probably overlooking something important.

Example: Steve is 2 years older than Andrew. The sum of their ages is 68. How old is Steve?

Answer: We know the least about Andrew, so make Andrew the unknown value. Let x = Andrew's age. Then Steve's age = $x + 2$. We know $(x + 2) + x = 68$. Then, $2x + 2 = 68$, $2x = 66$, $x = 33$. Are we done? No, because the problem asks for Steve's age, which is $x + 2$, or $33 + 2 = 35$.

There are unlimited kinds of algebra word problems; however, some kinds appear frequently. The above is an age problem comparing ages of two people; they can be tricky if the problem involves more than one-time period, such as ages 'two years ago.' We have previously discussed ratio problems and percent problems.

- Money problems involve two types of coins or two types of tickets; here, there can be a number of coins and the monetary value of each coin.
- Number problems may start out with, "the sum of two numbers is ..." or may involve consecutive numbers.
- Distance problems use the formula rate times time equals distance, and the key may be to recognize two objects are traveling the same distance or the same amount of time.
- Mixture problems involve combining things like peanuts and cashews to create a bag of mixed nuts.
- Digit problems involve manipulating unit digits, tens digits, etc. of numbers.
- Work problems involve several people working together to do a job.

Geometry problems and statistical problems are discussed in later chapters. This is not an exhaustive list.

It is important to check your answer for reasonability. If you have a negative number of coins, or an age of 400, there is probably something wrong. It is possible there is no realistic solution to a particular word problem; but hopefully not on this exam.

Example: If I have 70 coins in nickels and dimes for a total of $5.00, how many dimes do I have?

Answer: Let x = number of dimes and 70 - x = the number of nickels

$$(70 - x) * .05 + x * .10 = \$5.00$$

Multiply both sides by 100 to get rid of decimals. $(70 - x) * 5 + x * 10 = 500, 350 - 5x + 10x = 500, 5x = 150, x = 30.$

Check: 30 dimes plus 40 nickels equals: $30 * .10 + 40 * .05 = \$5.00$

Example: Find two consecutive, even, integers such that twice the smaller exceeds the larger by 20.

Answer: Let x = the smaller, x + 2 = the larger. $2x - (x+2) = 20; x - 2 = 20; x = 22, x + 2 = 24.$

Check: $2 * 22 - 24 = 20.$

Example: Suppose I drive for 3.5 hours, of which some is at 70-mph and some is at 30-mph. If the total distance is 225 miles, how much time was spent at each speed?

Answer: Let t = time at 70 mph, and $3.5 - t$ = time at 30 mph. Then $70t + 30(3.5 - t) = 225$. $70t + 105 - 30t = 225$, $40t = 120$, $t = 3$, $3.5 - t = .5$. (Be careful that units are consistent, such as time in hours and speed in mph.)

Example: If peanuts cost \$1.50 per pound and cashews cost \$3.00 per pound, how many pounds of each will be contained in a 150-pound mixture that can be sold for \$2.00 per pound?

Answer: Let x = pounds of peanuts, $150 - x$ be pounds of cashews. $1.50x + 3(150 - x) = 2 * 150$. $1.50x + 450 - 3x = 300$, $1.50x = 150$, $x = 100$, $150 - x = 50$.

Example: A 2-digit number has the property that the ten's digit is twice the unit's digit. If the number is reversed, the sum of the original number and the reversed number is 132. What is the original number?

Answer: Let u = the unit's digit of the original number, and 2u = ten's digit of original number. The original number equals (10 * 2u) + u, and the reversed number equals (10 * u) + 2u. Then (10 * 2u) + u + (10 * u) + 2u = 132; 20u + u + 10u + 2u = 33u = 132; u=4, the original number is 84.

Example: Ann can do a job in 3 hours. Bob can do the same job in 2 hours. How long would it take them to do the job if they worked together?

Answer: Let t = the time in hours to work together. Ann can do $\frac{1}{3}$ of the job in 1 hour, or t/3 = in t hours. Bob can do ½ of the job in 1 hour, or t/2 in t hours. If they work together they do the whole job, which equals 1. t/3 + t/2 = 1. 2t/6 + 3t/6 = 6/6, 5t = 6, t = 6/5.

Problems:

1. Aunt Ann is 4 times as old as nephew Ben. In 5 years, she will be 3 times as old as he will be then. How old are each of them now?

2. Cathy's and Dan's ages are in a ratio of 5:3. In 3 years, Dan will be 21. What was Cathy's age 5 years ago?

3. In 5 years from now, Ed and Fred's ages will be in a ratio of 3:5. The sum of their ages today is 46. How old was Ed 5 years ago?

4. Gina's and Harry's ages are in a ratio of 8:5, and Gina is 9 years older than Harry. What will the sum of their ages be in 6 years?

5. Ina's and Jack's ages are in a ratio of 4:3, and the product of their ages is 768. What will the ratio of their ages be in 8 years?

6. Kathy has $1.00 in dimes and nickels. She has 1 fewer nickels than dimes. How many of each does she have?

7. Laura has $3.00 in nickels, dimes, and quarters. She has twice as many nickels as dimes and 6 fewer quarters than dimes. How many of each does she have?

8. Mike has $3.00 consisting of 21 coins that are either dimes or quarters. How many of each are there?

9. A movie theatre sold 200 tickets. Some customers paid the regular price of $8 per ticket, and some customers had a coupon entitling them to a 25% discount. Total sales were $1,460. How many of each type of ticket were sold?

10. An organizer of a charity event charges $12 per ticket, but gets an overwhelmingly male audience. He thinks if he charges $12 for men, but gives a 30% discount for women, then he will get an audience of men to women in a ratio of 3:1. The organizer has fixed costs of $200, regardless of how many people attend. What is the fewest number of tickets he must sell so his net income will exceed $1,000?

11. In a 2-digit number, the ten's digit is twice the unit's digit. If 27 is subtracted from the number, then the result is the original number with its digits reversed. What is the original number?

12. The sum of the digits of a 2-digit number is 8. When 54 is subtracted from the number, its digits are reversed. What is the original number?

13. Nina drove 4 hours at 60 miles per hour and another 3 hours at 70 miles per hour. What was her average speed?

14. Oliver drove at an average speed of 60 mph from home to work, and an average speed of 40 mph from work to home. His total driving time was 3.75 hours. What is his 1-way distance from home to work?

15. Towns Mayberry and Springfield are 405 miles apart. At 5:00 p.m. a slow train leaves Mayberry for Springfield at 60 mph, and at the same time a fast train leaves Springfield for Mayberry at 75 mph. What time will the two trains meet?

16. Patty and Ralph are driving separately from Mayberry to Springfield. Patty left 4 hours earlier, but Ralph is driving 20 mph faster. It takes Ralph 12 hours to catch up with Patty. How fast is Patty driving?

17. You have quantities of a 10% acidity solution and a 35% acidity solution. How much of each should you mix to create 30 gallons of a 25% acidity solution?

18. Sam can do a job alone in 12 hours that Toni can do alone in 6 hours. How long will it take if they work together?

19. Uri can do a job alone in 8 hours. Uri and Vicki together can do it in 4 hours. How long would it take Vicki to do it alone?

20. One swimming pool pipe can fill the pool in 12 hours, while a second pipe can empty it in 16 hours. If both pipes are open, how long would it take to fill the pool?

Solutions to Problems:

1. Let x = Ben now, 4x = Ann now. In 5 years, Ben

   will be x + 5, Ann will be 4x + 5, and

   (4x + 5)/(x + 5) = 3. Then 4x + 5 = 3(x + 5) =

   3x + 15, x = 10, 4x = 40.

2. Let x = proportionality constant now, so Cathy's

   and Dan's ages now are 5x and 3x.

   3x + 3 = 21, so x = 6. Their ages now are 30

   and 18; 5 years ago, Cathy was 25.

3. Let x = proportionality constant in 5 years, so Ed's

   and Fred's ages in 5 years are 3x and 5x.

   Today their ages are 3x - 5 and 5x - 5;

   (3x - 5) + (5x - 5) = 46, so 8x -10 = 46,

   8x = 56, x=7; ages in 5 years are 3 * 7 = 21

and 5 * 7 = 35; ages today are 16 and 30;

and 5 years ago, Ed was 11.

4. Let x = proportionality constant now, so their ages

are 8x and 5x, and 8x − 5x = 9, 3x = 9, x = 3,

so they are 8 * 3 = 24 and 5 * 3 = 15 now. In 6

years they will be 30 and 21, with a sum of 51.

5. Let x = proportionality constant now, so their ages

are 4x and 3x, and we know (4x)(3x) = 768.

So $12x^2$ = 768, x^2 = 64, x = 8 (and also -8, but

reject as not possible for ages). Their ages

now are 4 * 8 = 32 and 3 * 8 = 24. In 8 years

their ratio will be (32 + 8)/((24 + 8) = $^{40}/_{32}$ = $^{5}/_{4}$.

6. Let D = number of dimes, and D-1 = number of

nickels. Then .10D + .05(D-1) = 1.00, .15D -

.05 = 1, .15D = 1.05, D = 7, D-1=6.

7. Let D = number of dimes, 2D = number of nickels, and D-6 = number of quarters. Then .05(2D) + .10D + .25(D-6) = 3.00. .10D + .10D + .25D - 1.5 = 3, .45D = 4.5, D=10. Then nickels = 20, and quarters = 4.

8. Let D = number of dimes, and 21-D = number of quarters. Then .10D + .25(21-D) = 3.00. .10D + 5.25 - .25D = 3, .15D = 2.25, D = 15, 21-D=6. Then 15 dimes and 6 quarters.

9. A 25% discount on an $8.00 ticket is a discount of .25 * 8 = 2, so the discounted ticket is 8 - 2 = 6. Let x = number of $8.00 tickets, and 200 - x = number of $6.00 tickets. 8x + 6(200 - x) = 1,460. 8x + 1,200 - 6x = 1,480, 2x = 260, x = 130, 200 - x = 70. So, 130 $8.00 tickets and 70 $6.00 tickets.

10. A 30% discount on an $12.00 ticket is.30 * 12 = $3.60, so the discounted ticket is $12.00 - $3.60 = $8.40. Let x = number of $8.40 tickets, and 3x = number of $12.00 tickets. Then, $8.40x + 12(3x) - 200 > $1,000.00; 8.4x + 36x > $1,200.00, 44.4x > $1,200.00, x > 27.027 (rounded). If x = 28, 3x = 84, sum = 112 tickets.

11. Let U = the unit's digit and let 2U = the ten's digit. The number is 10(2U) + U, or 21U. 21U - 27 = 10U + 2U; 21U - 27 = 12U; 9U = 27; U = 3. The number is 21U = 63.

12. Let U = the unit's digit, and 8 - U = the ten's digit. The number is 10(8 - U) + U, or 80 − 9U. The reversed number is 10U + (8 - U), or 9U + 8. (80 - 9U) − 54 = 9U + 8, 26 - 9U = 9U + 8; 18 = 18U; U = 1; 8 − U = 7, original number is 71.

13. Rate * Time = Distance, Rate = Distance/Time. Total distance equals (4 hours * 60 mph) + (3 hours * 70 mph) = 240 + 210 miles = 450 miles. Total time = 4 hours + 3 hours = 7 hours. Average speed = 450 miles / 7 hours = 64.3 mph (rounded).

14. Let t = number of hours from home to work, and 3.75 - t = number of hours from work to home. The distance from home to work is 60t, the distance from work to home is 40(3.75 - t), and these distances are equal. 60t = 40(3.75 - t). 60t = 150 - 40t, 100t = 150, t = 1.5. Then distance = 60t = 60 * 1.5 = 90.

15. Let t = travel time of each train. The slow train travels a distance D = 60t, and the fast train travels a distance 75t; 60t + 75t = 405; 135t = 405, t = 3; 3 hours from 5:00 p.m. is 8:00 p.m.

16. Let R = Patty's speed, and R + 20 = Ralph's speed. Patty is driving for 4 + 12 = 16 hours, at a distance D = 16R. Ralph is driving 12 hours, at a distance D = 12(R + 20). The distances are the same, so 16R = 12(R + 20). 16R = 12R + 240, 4R = 240. R = 60. <u>Check</u>: Patty drove a distance D = 16 * 60 = 960. Ralph drove a distance D = 12 * 80 = 960.

17. Let x = gallons of 10%, and 30 - x = gallons of 35%; .10x + .35(30 - x) = .25 * 30; .10x + 10.5 - .35x = 7.5; .25x = 3; x = 12; 30-x = 18. <u>Check</u>: (.10 * 12 + .35 * 18)/(12 + 18) = .25.

18. Let t = time to work together. Sam can do $^1/_{12}$ of the job in 1 hour, or t/12 = in t hours. Toni can do $^1/_6$ of the job in 1 hour, or t/6 in t hours. If they work together they do the whole job, which equals 1. t/12 + t/6 = 1. t/12 + 2t/12 = 12/12, 3t = 12, t = 4 hours.

19. Let t = time for Vicki alone. $^4/_8$ + 4/t = 1.

    The LCD is 8t. 4t / 8t + 4 * 8 / 8t = 8t / 8t,

    4t + 32 = 8t, 4t = 32, t = 8.

20. Let t = time to work together. t/12 - t/16 = 1.

    The LCD is 48. 4t / 48 - 3t / 48 = 48 / 48,

    t = 48.

Chapter 4

Geometry

Geometry is a word derived from the ancient Greek words for measurement of the earth. It began in Greece about 600 B.C. to deal with practical problems of lengths, areas, and volumes. More generally it is the branch of math dealing with shapes, sizes, and position of figures. With the development of an xy coordinate system, there is an overlap between geometry and algebra; geometric figures can be drawn in an xy coordinate system, and problems in geometry are sometimes handled with algebra.

When looking at geometric figures, do not make assumptions such as sides are equal, lines are parallel, an angle is 90^0, the figures are drawn to scale, etc.

A line continues infinitely in both directions. A ray is a part of a line that begins at one endpoint called a vertex and then continues infinitely in one direction. When two rays intersect, they form an angle. An angle is measured in degrees (^{0}), usually counterclockwise between 0^0 and 360^0. An acute angle is greater than 0^0 and less than 90^0. A right angle is 90^0 and may be designated with a small square (see sample following).

An obtuse angle is greater than 90^0 and less than 180^0. A straight angle is 180^0. A reflex angle is greater than 180^0 and less than 360^0. An angle may be denoted $\angle$. Two angles are complementary when they add to 90^0. Two angles are supplementary when they add to 180^0.

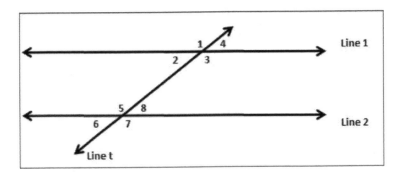

Two angles are congruent angles when they have the same measure in degrees, and then they are called equal. When two parallel lines are crossed by another line called the transversal, they create eight angles. Corresponding angles are angles that occupy the same relative position at each intersection; corresponding angles are equal. So $\angle 1$ = $\angle 5$, $\angle 3$ = $\angle 7$, $\angle 4$ = $\angle 8$, $\angle 2$ = $\angle 6$. Opposite angles are opposite each other when two lines intersect, such as $\angle 6$ and $\angle 8$, and they are equal.

If the measure of any of the eight angles is known, the other seven angles can be calculated.

Example: In the diagram above, if lines 1 and 2 are parallel and if $\angle 4 = 32^0$, then $\angle 2 = 32^0$ because these are opposite angles. $\angle 1$ is supplementary to both $\angle 4$ and $\angle 2$, so $\angle 1 = 180^0 - 32^0 = 148^0$. $\angle 3$ also equals 148^0. $\angle 6$ and $\angle 8$ will each equal 32^0, and $\angle 5$ and $\angle 7$ will each equal 148^0.

Two figures are congruent if their corresponding angles are equal and their corresponding sides are equal. The congruent symbol is $\cong$, as in $\triangle$ ABC $\cong$ $\triangle$ DEF. Two figures are similar if their corresponding angles are equal and their corresponding sides are proportional. The similarity symbol is ~, as in $\triangle$ GHI ~ $\triangle$ JKL.

A figure may be transformed into another congruent figure by the motions of reflection (flipping), rotation (turning), or translation (sliding, with neither a flip nor a turn). A figure may be transformed into another similar figure by dilation, which includes enlarging it or reducing it proportionally.

A polygon is a closed figure made up of line segments. A triangle is a 3-sided polygon, and the sum of its interior angles is 180^0. The area of a triangle equals ½ base times height, and the perimeter is the sum of the three sides. The sum of any two sides of a triangle is greater than the third side (Triangle Inequality). An equilateral triangle is when all three sides are equal, an isosceles triangle is when two sides are equal (and there will be two equal angles opposite those equal sides), and a scalene triangle is when all three sides are unequal. An acute triangle is when each interior angle is less than 90^0, a right triangle is when one angle is 90^0, and an obtuse triangle is when one interior angle is greater than 90^0.

The Pythagorean Theorem says in a right triangle, the sum of the squares of the two shorter sides equals the square of the larger side called the hypotenuse.

A quadrilateral is a 4-sided polygon, and the sum of its interior angles is 360^0. A square has four equal sides and four equal 90^0 angles. A rectangle has four equal 90^0 angles, but only two pairs of equal sides. A parallelogram has two pairs of parallel - equal sides, and opposite angles are equal. A trapezoid has only one pair of parallel sides. Less common are a rhombus, which is a parallelogram with four equal sides, but no right angles, and a kite which has two pairs of equal sides adjacent to each other. A quadrilateral may also have all four sides unequal.

The area of a rectangle is length times width. The area of a parallelogram is base times height (which is an analogous formula). The area of a trapezoid is ½ height * ($base_1$ + $base_2$); this is also an analogous formula, and can be thought of as the parallelogram formula, except here we are taking the average of the two bases.

A circle is a closed curved figure – all of whose points are an equal distance from the center. A line segment from the center to any point on the circle is called the radius represented by r. A line segment with endpoints on the circle and passing through the center is called the diameter d; $d = 2r$. The perimeter of a circle is called the circumference C; $C = \pi d = 2\pi r$, where π is an irrational number. The area A of a circle equals πr^2. A central angle is the angle formed by two radii, up to a maximum of 360°. When two points lie on a circle, the curved line connecting them is called an arc. A sector is the part of a circle enclosed by two radii and their arc. A tangent line touches the circle at one and only point, and it is perpendicular to the radius that touches that same point.

Three-dimensional figures have volume (amount of space the figure occupies) and surface area (sum of the areas of each two-dimensional surface). Volume of a rectangular solid equals length times width times height. Sometimes volume can be thought of as piling two-dimensional figures on top of each other. Volume of a cylinder equals $\pi r^2 h$, which can be thought of as piling h circles on top of each other. Surface area of a cylinder equals $2\pi rh$, which can be thought of unraveling the paper covering of a can having height h and width equal to the circumference of the can; this surface area formula excludes the areas of the top and bottom which if needed equal $2\pi r^2$.

A cone has volume equal to $1/3$ of a cylinder, so $(1/3)\pi r^2 h$. A pyramid has one base, and all sides lead from the base to join in a point at the top (picture the Egyptian pyramids). A prism has two identical parallel bases joined together at the sides (picture a triangular tent, where the bases are front and back triangles, and there are three rectangles including the floor).

A pyramid with three triangular lateral surfaces plus a base has volume equal to $(1/3)$(base area) (height). A triangular prism has volume equal to (base area)(height). A sphere is a three-dimensional circle with volume equal $(4/3)\pi r^3$, and surface area equal $4\pi r^2$. In calculating areas of irregularly-shaped figures, feel free to draw extra lines to create regular figures.

Problems:

1. Let lines 1 and 2 be parallel, $\angle CAB = 60^0$, and

$\angle ABC = 70^0$. Calculate the measure of

$\angle BCD$ and $\angle DCE$.

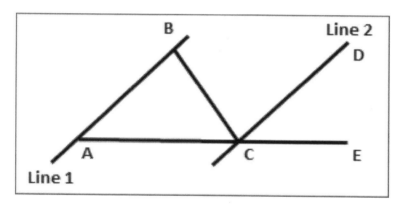

2. Let lines 1 and 2 be parallel. Calculate x and y.

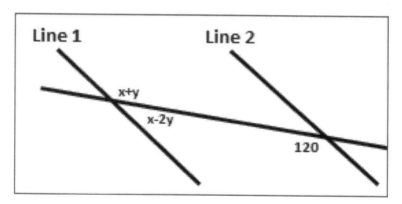

3. Suppose quadrilaterals ABCD and EFGH are similar, with their sides in the ratio of 3:1. What is the ratio of their perimeters? What is the ratio of their areas?

4. In the diagram below, line segments DE and BC are parallel, AD=20, DB=x, AE=y, EC=15, DE=14, and BC=21. Find x and y.

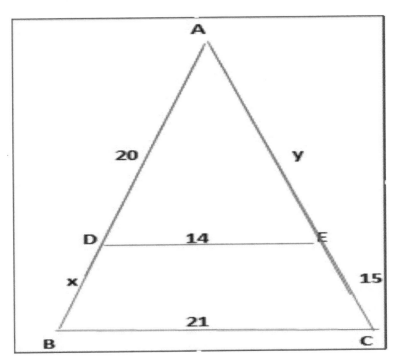

5. A building casts a 60-foot shadow from the sun at the same time that a 6-foot man casts a 5-foot shadow. How tall is the building?

6. Let Δ ABC be a triangle in the first quadrant as show below. What are the coordinates of Δ A'B'C' after Δ ABC has been reflected in the y-axis?

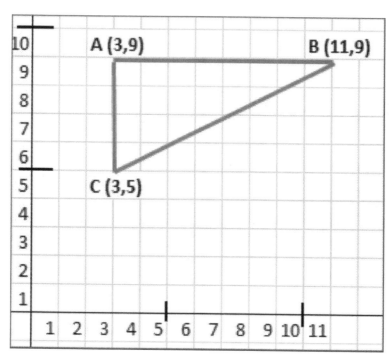

7. In the above diagram, what are the coordinates of

    Δ A"B"C" after Δ ABC has been reflected in

    the x-axis?

8. Let Δ ABC be a triangle in the first quadrant as

    show below. Which triangle if any is a rotation

    of Δ ABC?

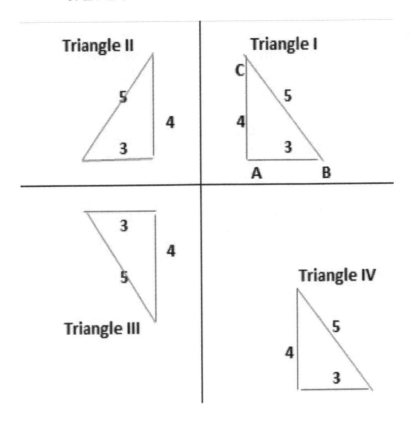

9. A local pizza store sells a medium pizza (12-inch diameter) for $12.00, and it sells a large pizza (14-inch diameter) for $14.00. Which is the better buy?

10. A cylinder with radius of 4 and height of 4 has its radius doubled, with the height unchanged. What is the ratio of the volume of the larger cylinder to the volume of the smaller cylinder?

11. A spherical balloon of radius of 2 inches, filled with water, sits half inside and half outside a hollow cone having radius of 2 inches and a height of 8 inches. If the water leaks into the cone, is there enough space in the cone to handle all the water?

12. Find the area and perimeter of the following figure.

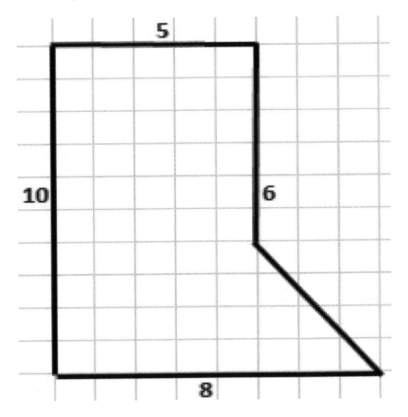

13. Which set of numbers may represent the lengths

of the sides of a triangle?

    a) {9,8,1}

    b) {3,7,4}

    c) {3,9,8}

    d) {2,4,9}.

14. What is the area of a right triangle with 1 leg

equal to $2\sqrt{3}$ and hypotenuse equal to 4?

15. What is the measure of the central angle of a

circular clock formed by the hands of the clock

at 4:30?

16. A circular clock has a diameter of 6. What is the

area of the sector formed by the hands of the

clock at 4:30?

17. The width of a rectangle is 4 less than the length.

The perimeter is 32. What is the area?

18. The following diagram represents a triangular prism with two parallel triangular bases. Calculate the volume of the prism.

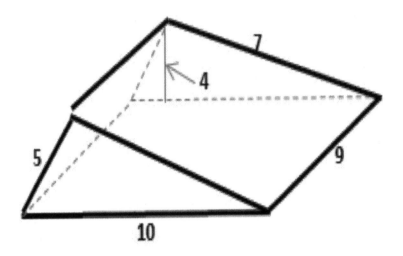

Solutions to Problems:

1. $\angle ABC$ and $\angle BCD$ are a pair of alternate interior

   angles, so $\angle BCD = 70^0$ and $\angle DCE = 180^0-$

   $50^0-70^0 = 60^0$.

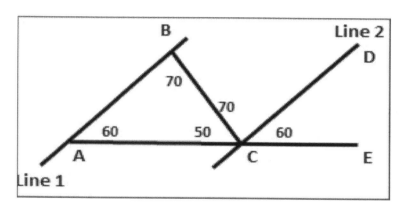

2. $x + y = 120$, because these are a pair of alternate

   interior angles; $(x + y) + (x - 2y) = 2x - y = 180$,

   because these are supplementary. Add $x + y =$

   120 to $2x - y = 180$, so $3x = 300$, $x = 100$; $x + y$

   $= 120$, so $100 + y = 120$, $y = 20$.

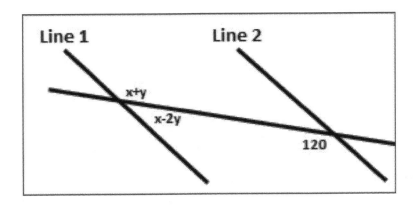

3. The ratio of their perimeters is the same 3:1. The ratio of the areas is $3^2:1^2$, or 9:1. You could test this in a specific case such as a 3 x 6 rectangle and 1 x 2 rectangle.

4. Because of the parallel lines, corresponding angles are equal, so $\triangle ADE \sim \triangle ABC$. Therefore, the lengths of corresponding sides are proportional, in the ratio 14:21, or 2:3. Then $20/(20 + x) = 2/3$ and $y/(y + 15) = 2/3$. The first equation gives x=10, and the second equation gives y = 30. (see following diagram)

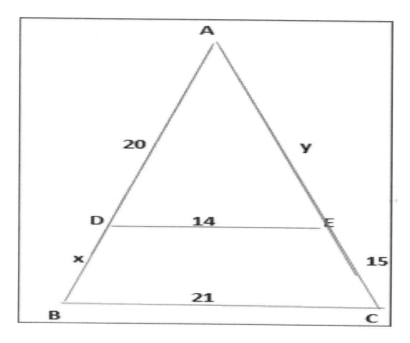

5. The building and the man can be thought of as

   parallel lines, creating similar triangles. Let h =

   height of building. 5/60 = 6/h, 5h = 360, h = 72.

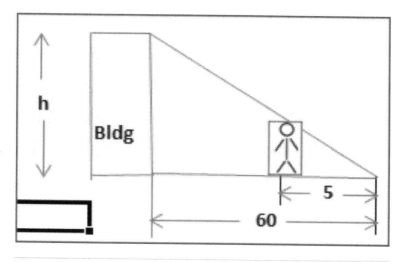

6. A reflection in the y-axis changes each point (x,y)

   into (-x,y). So, A' = (-3,9), B' = (-11,9), and C'

   = (-3,5).

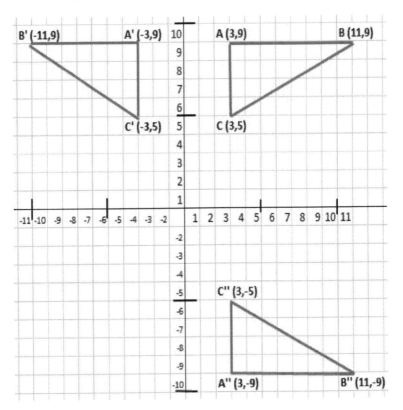

7. A reflection in the x-axis changes each point (x,y)

   into (x, -y). So A" = (3,-9), B" = (11,-9), C" =

   (3,-5).

8. Triangle III is a 180° degree rotation of Triangle I about the origin.

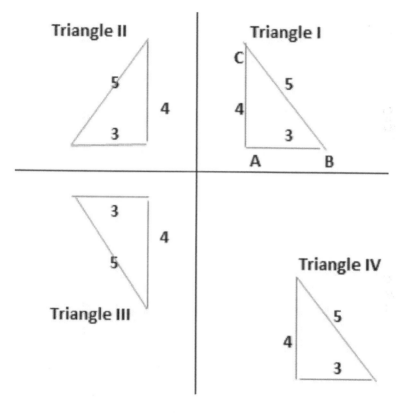

9. Compare price per square inch: Price/ πr^2.

Medium is $12/(\pi 6^2) = 1/(3\pi)$. Large = $14/(\pi 7^2)$

= $2/(7\pi)$. $1/3 > 2/7$ (ignore the π term which is

the same for both), so large costs less per

square inch.

10. $V = \pi r^2 h$. Ratio $= \pi 8^2 4 \,/\, \pi 4^2 4 = {}^{64}/_{16} = 4$.

11. Volume of sphere $= (^4/_3) \pi r^3 = (^4/_3) \pi 2^3 = (^{32}/_3) \pi$;

    volume of cone $= (^1/_3) \pi r^2 h = (^1/_3) \pi 2^2 8 =$

    $(^{32}/_3)\pi$. The volumes are equal.

12. Draw the line segment shown below as a dashed
    line, creating a right triangle. The area of the
    rectangle is 5 * 10 = 50, and the area of the
    triangle is ½ * 4 * 3 = 6, so the total area is 56.
    By the Pythagorean Theorem, the hypotenuse
    of the right triangle equals $\sqrt{(3^2 + 4^2)} = 5$. The
    perimeter is 10 + 5 + 6 + 5 + 8 = 34.

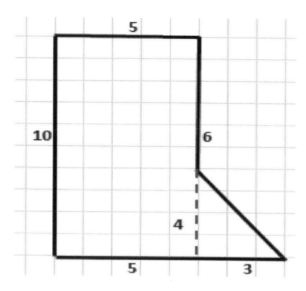

13. The sum of any two sides of a triangle is greater than the third side. Only C {3,9,8} has the property that every two numbers is greater than the third number.

14. The Pythagorean Theorem says $a^2 + b^2 = c^2$, where c is the hypotenuse. Let a = the unknown leg. Then $a^2 + (2\sqrt{3})^2 = 4^2$, $a^2 + 4*3 = 16$, $a^2 = 4$, a = 2.

Area = ½ base * height = ½ * 2 * 2√3 = 2√3.

15. There are 12 numbers on a clock, and 360 degrees to a circle, so each number represents 360/12 = 30 degrees. At 4:30, the small hand is on 4.5 and the big hand is on 6, a difference of 1.5. This 1.5 * 30 degrees = 45 degrees.

16. The radius is 3, and the area of the circle is πr^2, or $\pi 3^2$, or 9π; 4:30 represents 45°, or $^{45}/_{360}$, or $^1/_8$ of the circle. The area of the sector is $(^1/_8)(9\pi)$ or $9\pi/8$.

17. Let x = length and x-4 = width. Then 32 = 2x + 2(x - 4), 32 = 4x - 8, x = 10, x - 4 = 6, area = 10 * 6 = 60.

18. Volume = (base area)(height). The base is the 5 by 7 by 10 triangle, with a height of 4, and whose area = ½ 10 * 4 = 20. The height of the prism is 9; Volume = (20)(9) = 180.

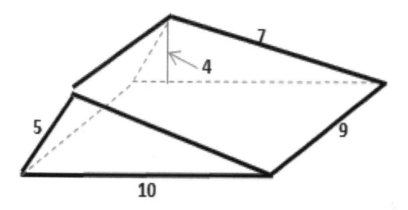

Chapter 5

Statistics and Probability

Unlike the previous types of math that date back thousands of years, probability and statistics are more recent branches of mathematics. Probability is the relative likelihood of something happening. Probability dates back to 1654, to a gambler's dispute between two French mathematicians. Statistics is the subject of planning experiments, and then obtaining, summarizing, presenting, analyzing, and interpreting data, and then drawing conclusions. Although collecting data goes back to ancient times, some authors say statistics began in 1662 with the production of a mortality table by two British mathematicians.

Probability

For this exam, you should be familiar with a deck of 52 playing cards. There are four suits: diamonds (red), hearts (red), spades (♠ black), and clubs (♣ black). Within each suit there are 13 cards: Ace, 2, 3, 4, 5, 6, 7, 8, 9, 10, Jack, Queen, King. Jack, Queen, and King are called picture cards. You should also be familiar with dice, whose singular is die; a die is a 6-sided cube with each face having a whole number of dots from 1 to 6.

If we are interested in some event 'A' that can occur in a variety of different ways, the probability of A, denoted P(A), equals the (number of ways A can occur)/ (number of ways all events can occur). Example: Suppose 1,000 Praxis core math students were surveyed, and 850 said the exam is hard. Now suppose one of those 1000 students is selected at random. The probability that this randomly selected person said the exam is hard equals 850/1000 = .85.

An event A may either occur, or it may not occur, and there is no third possibility. P(not A) = 1 - P(A).

Probabilities are between 0 and 1; an impossible event has a probability of zero, and a certain event has probability equal to 1. If A and B are events, then P(A or B) = P(A) + P(B) - P(A and B).

This is illustrated visually with a Venn Diagram where each event is illustrated as a circle. A or B is the region covered by the two circles, including the overlapping area, but the overlapping area should not be counted twice. Note in the diagram there are four regions: A, B, A and B, and not (A or B).

Two-Circle Venn Diagram

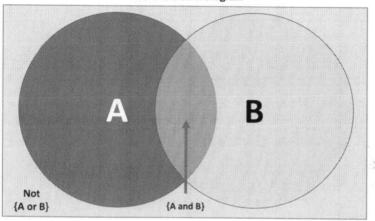

Example: Suppose there are 100 students: 55 are taking English, 35 are taking math, and 10 are taking both. If a student is chosen at random, then P(English) = 55/100, P(math) = 35/100, P(English and math) = 10/100, P(English or math) = 55/100 + 35/100 - 10/100 = 80/100, and P(neither English nor math) = 1-80/100 = 20/100. Note that P(English or math) does not equal 55/100 + 35/100 because that would double count the 10 students taking both.

If two events are independent, the occurrence of one event does not affect the probability of the other event, and we have P(A and B) = P(A) * P(B). If two events are not independent, then the probability of the second event must be calculated recognizing that the first event has occurred.

When an item is sampled and then replaced where it could be sampled again, the selections are independent events. When an item is sampled and not replaced, these are not independent events, and the probability of the second event must be calculated recognizing the first event has occurred.

Example: One card is selected at random from a deck of 52 playing cards, and then a second card is selected at random. What is the probability of selecting a black picture card first, and then selecting a black picture card second, if:

a. the first card is replaced in the deck after it is selected; and
b. the first card is not replaced in the deck after it is selected?

Answer: There are six black picture cards (Jack, Queen, and King, for each of two suits: clubs and spades), out of 52 cards. The probability of the first card being a black picture card is $6/52$.

a. If the first card is replaced in the deck after it is selected, then the probability of the second card being a black picture card is also $6/52$, and the probability of the first black picture and the second black picture = $(6/52) * (6/52)$.
b. If the first card is not replaced in the deck after it is selected, then the probability of the second card being a black picture card is $5/51$, and the probability of the first black picture and the second black picture = $(6/52) * (5/51)$.

When events are independent, they have no memory of what has occurred in the past. If a coin is fair, then its probability of landing heads on any toss is 50%, even if it has landed tails 10 times in a row. If it is tossed many times, in the long run its number of heads will be very close to 50%. Unless you are told otherwise, assume that a coin is fair.

A coin has two outcomes: H or T. When it is flipped three times, there are two outcomes for the first flip, times two outcomes for the second flip, times two outcomes for the third flip, or $2 * 2 * 2 = 2^3 = 8$ outcomes. Note for example that HTT and THT are different outcomes.

A probability distribution is a table or graph with all possible outcomes and their probabilities. The sum of all such probabilities equals 1. (If you are creating a probability distribution and the sum is not 1, then there is an error.) For example, if a fair coin is flipped three times, there may be 0 heads, 1 head, 2 heads, or 3 heads.

Write out all the possible outcomes:

Number of Heads	Outcomes	Number of Outcomes	Probability

Number of Heads	Outcomes	Number of Outcomes	Probability
0	TTT	1	1/8
1	HTT, THT, TTH	3	3/8
2	HHT, HTH, THH	3	3/8
3	TTT	1	1/8
Totals		8	1

The probability distribution as a table is the first and last columns above. As a graph, it looks like the following:

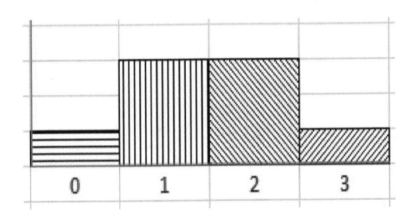

A die has six outcomes: 1, 2, 3, 4, 5, or 6. There are six outcomes for the first die, times six outcomes for the second die, or 6 * 6 = 6^2 = 36 outcomes. (1,3) and (3,1) are different outcomes. When two dice are rolled, their sums range from 2 to 12. You can write all 36 outcomes and calculate, for example, there are three ways to roll a sum of 4:1 and 3, 3 and 1, and 2 and 2, so P(4) = $^3/_{36}$.

Statistics

Statistics is the subject of planning experiments, and then obtaining, summarizing, presenting, analyzing, and interpreting data and drawing conclusions. Sometimes we have data for the entire population of interest, such as all 500 students at Millard Fillmore Elementary School. Other times we may want data from a sample, which is a sub-collection of the larger population, such as 50 of those 500 students. Ideally in selecting a sample, we want a random sample, so that every population member has an equal probability of being selected, and so the sample is reasonably representative of the population. If we selected the 50 oldest students, the 50 students with the highest grades, or even the first 50 students walking through the door, these would not be random samples; instead if we used a process such as putting all 500 names in a hat, thoroughly mixing the names, and then randomly selecting 50 names, then this would be a random and representative sample.

When there are a large number of data values summarize the data numerically or graphically to make the data easier to analyze. Numerically, we measure both the center of the data and the variation of the data (how much the data vary around the center). We measure the center with mean, median, and mode. Mean or average equals the sum of the data values divided by the number of data values. Median requires the data be sorted from lowest to highest; if there is an odd number of data values then the median is the middle value, and if there is an even number of data values then the median is the average of the two middle values. Mode equals the data value that occurs the most number of times; there may be a tie and therefore several modes, or there may be no modes.

Percentile is a measure of what percent of the sorted data is lower than a particular value. The 75th percentile value, also called third quartile, is the value such that 75% of the data values are lower than that value. Median, also called second quartile, is the value such that 50% of the data values are lower than that value. The 25th percentile value, also called first quartile, is the value such that 25% of the data values are lower than that value.

We measure the variability with range, standard deviation, and interquartile range. Range equals maximum value minus minimum value. Standard deviation represents the average amount that values vary from the mean, but the actual calculation is beyond the scope of this exam.

Interquartile Range (IQR) = third quartile minus first quartile. An outlier is a data value that is a much lower or much higher than the next data value; for example, if 9 houses sold for about $250,000 each and the 10th sold for $2.5 million, that last house sold is an outlier.

A boxplot is a graph summarizing all the data by showing the five values' minimum, first quartile, median, third quartile, and maximum.

Example: Calculate mean, median, mode, range, and IQR for the data {8, 3, 6, 10, 4, 1, 10, 9}, and draw the boxplot.

Answer:
Mean = (8 + 3 + 6 + 10 + 4 + 1 + 10 + 9)/8 = 6.375.
For median, sort the data: {1, 3, 4, **6, 8**, 9, 10, 10};
there is an even number of data values, so the median = (6+8)/2 = 7.
The mode is 10.
The range is 10 – 1 = 9.
The third quartile is the middle of {8, 9, 10, 10} = 9.5.
The first quartile is the middle of {1, 3, 4, 6} = 3.5.
The IQR equals 9.5 - 3.5 = 6.

Boxplot:

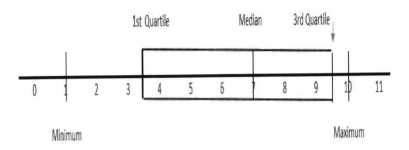

A stem-and-leaf plot is a graph summarizing all the data by separating each data value into its leftmost digit and its rightmost digit.

Example: Draw a stem-and-leaf plot for the data {18, 35, 25, 21, 24, 21, 23, 24, 18, 32, 38}, and use it to find the median and mode.

Answer: Sort the data. The median is the 6th value, 24. There are three modes: 18, 21, and 24.

Stem	Leaf
1	8,8
2	1,1,3,4,4,5
3	2,5,8

When you have two variables that exist as ordered pairs, you can draw the ordered pairs as points on an xy-coordinate system and ask whether the points are close to forming a straight line or not. If the points are close to forming a straight line, we say a correlation exists. If the straight line has positive slope, then as x values increase the y values generally increase, and we say there is positive correlation. If the straight line has negative slope, then as x values increase the y values generally decrease, and we say there is negative correlation.

The closer the points are to a straight line, the stronger is the correlation. If the points are not at all close to forming a straight line, we say no correlation exists. It is easy in real life to find data exhibiting a strong correlation, such as subway prices and pizza prices, but this does not tell us that one variable causes the other.

There are many ways to display data in graphs and many questions that can be asked. Be sure to understand the title and axis names of any graph.

Example: In the following graph, which child had the greatest percentage growth?

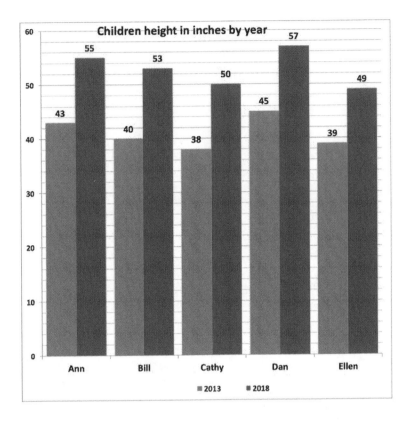

Answer: You need to calculate each child's percent change. Cathy: $(^{50}/_{38} - 1) * 100\% = 31.6\%$.

Problems:

1. Use the following table to calculate the probability that if a person is chosen at random, that person will be:

   a. Female
   b. Female currently unmarried
   c. Female or currently married
   d. Female, given the person is currently married.

	Currently unmarried	Currently married	Total
Male	25	65	90
Female	30	80	110
Total	55	145	200

2. Two dice are rolled. Calculate the probability that each die will show a prime number less than 5.

3. Two cards are randomly selected from a 52-card deck. Calculate the probability that neither is a black picture card.

4. Use the following graph. If a person is chosen at random, calculate the probability the person:

   a. Does not carry 4 or fewer keys

   b. Carries 8 or fewer keys

   c. Carries 9 or 10 keys or is a woman.

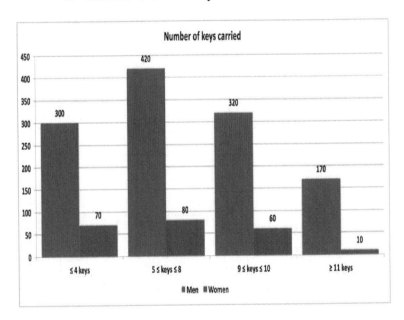

5. In a state where recreational use of marijuana is legal, insurance companies are concerned about its potential incidence in auto accidents. Suppose the probability of an accident is .10, the probability of using marijuana is .30, and the probability of using marijuana or having an accident is .35. Calculate the probability of using marijuana and having an accident.

6. Suppose the probability of a serious hurricane in any year is .10, and suppose the probability is independent from year-to-year. What is the probability of at least one serious hurricane in 10 years?

7. When two dice are rolled, what is the probability their sum will be 6?

8. Fifty people were surveyed as to how many movies they saw in a year, with the following result. If a person from this sample was randomly selected, what is the probability that person saw more than 20 movies?

Number of movies	0	1 through 5	6 through 10	11 through 15	16 through 20
Number of people	7	15	10	8	7

9. Fifty-one people were surveyed as to how many books they read in a month, with the results in the following table. Use the table to calculate the mean, median, and mode. If 1 of the 7 people actually read 40 books rather than 4, which among mean, median, and mode would change the most from your first calculation?

Number of books read	0	1	2	3	4
Number of people	8	16	11	9	7

10. Use the following boxplot to calculate the ratio of the interquartile range to the maximum.

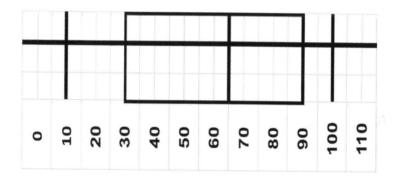

11. A psychologist is testing students' driving ability while texting with a driving simulator to determine how many simulated accidents they have, with the following results. Based on the following graph, is the distribution of accidents symmetrical or skewed, and which is larger: median or mean?

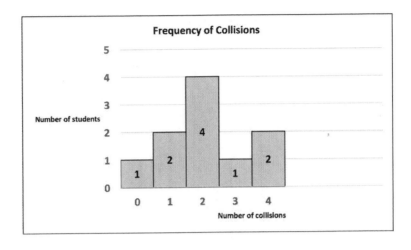

12. Suppose a cow has a square 1x1 field to graze in. Let the area be drawn on an xy coordinate system as defined by x=0, y=0, x=1, and y=1. Draw the line y = -2x+1 within this 1x1 field, which then divides the field into a smaller area and a larger area. Assume the cow wanders randomly within this field. What is the probability at a single point in time that the cow will be in the larger of the two areas?

13. In a 6-team league, suppose the probabilities of each of the six teams winning the championship are as follows. Calculate the probabilities of winning for each of the Anteaters, the Elephants, and the Ferrets.

Team	Probability
Anteaters	x + .05
Barn Owls	.30
Crocodiles	.05
Deer	.20
Elephants	2x
Ferrets	x

14. The Hamsters and the Rodents are two football teams that play the same number of games. The following is a graph of their number of points per game and the number of games that they scored each number of points. What can you conclude about their means and standard deviations of their number of points per game?

Hamsters vs Rodents

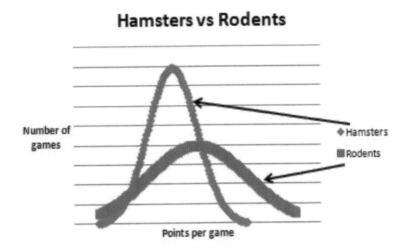

15. Which of the following graphs exhibits the

strongest correlation?

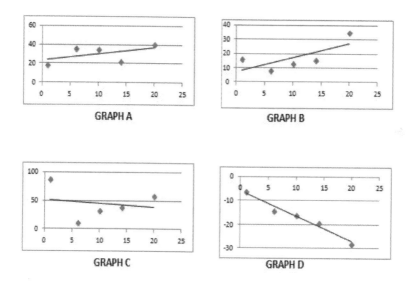

16. Twenty people aged 80 and over who have

smoked cigarettes for fifty or more years are selected

at random from a hospital database. A graph is

drawn comparing number of years of smoking versus

severity if any of lung cancer. The graph exhibits a

strong but not perfect positive correlation. Does this

study demonstrate smoking causes cancer? Either

answer yes, or give a reason why your answer is no.

Solutions to Problems:

1.

	Currently unmarried	Currently married	Total
Male	25	65	90
Female	30	80	110
Total	55	145	200

a. P(Female) = 110/200. b. P(Female currently unmarried) = 30/200. c. P(Female or currently married) = (110+145-80)/200 = 175/200. d. P(Female, given that the person is currently married) = 80/145.

2. There are six possible rolls of one die, of which 2 and 3 are primes less than 5; P(1st roll is prime less than 5) = 2/6; P(2nd roll is prime less than 5) = 2/6; and P(1st and 2nd less than 5) = (2/6)* (2/6) = 4/36.

3. There are six black picture cards. P(1ˢᵗ card is not a black picture card) = (52-6)/52 = 46/52. (2ⁿᵈ card is not a black picture card) = (51-6)/51 = 45/51. (1ˢᵗ and 2ⁿᵈ are not black picture cards) = (46/52) * (45/51) = 2070/2652.

4.

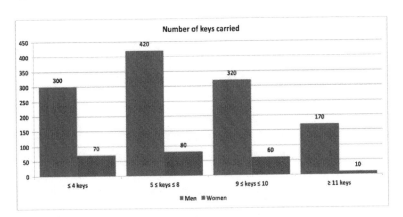

There are (300 + 70 + 420 + 80 + 320 + 60 + 170 + 10) = 1430 people.

   a. P(Does not carry 4 or fewer keys) =

      1- P(Carries 4 or fewer keys) =

      1- 370/1430 =1060/1430

   b. P(Carries 8 or fewer keys) =

      (300 + 70 + 420 + 80)/1430 = 870/1430

c. P(Carries 9 or 10 keys or is a woman) =

((320 + 60) + (70 + 80 + 60 + 10) - 60)/1430

= 540/1430.

5. Let A = accident, M = marijuana. P(A or M) = P(A) + P(M) - P(A and M), .35 = .10 + .30 - P(A and M), so P(A and M) = .05.

6. The probability of at least 1, equals 1 minus the probability of none. Let H = hurricane in any year. P(H) = .10, P(not H) = 1 - P(H) = 1 - .10 = .90. P(no H in 10 years) = .90 * .90 * .90 * .90 * .90 * .90 * .90 * .90 * .90 * .90 = $.90^{10}$ = .349. P(at least 1) = 1 - .349 = .651

7. There are 6 * 6 = 36 outcomes from rolling two dice. There are five ways to get a sum of 6: {(1,5), (2,4), (3,3), (4,2), (5,1)}. The probability is 5/36.

8. Fifty people were surveyed, but only

   $(7 + 15 + 10 + 8 + 7) = 47$ are in the table.

   The remaining 3 must have seen more than 20

   movies. Probability = $^3/_{50}$.

9. Mean = $(0 * 8 + 1 * 16 + 2 * 11 + 3 * 9 + 4 * 7)/51$

   = 1.82. Think of this is having to add eight

   zeros, plus 16 ones, etc. The median is the

   middle of 51 numbers, which is the 26th

   number; by accumulating the number of people

   you can see the 26th number occurs in the row

   for books = 2, so median = 2. The mode

   occurs at books = 1. If one large outlier were

   included, the mean would change the most.

Books	People	Books x People	Cumulative People
0	8	0	8
1	16	16	24
2	11	22	35
3	9	27	44
4	7	28	51
Total	51	93	

10. IQR = third quartile minus first quartile =

90 - 30 = 60. Maximum = 100.

IQR/maximum = 60/100.

11.

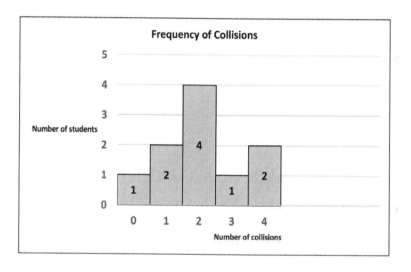

The graph is not symmetrical. The mean equals

(0 * 1 + 1 * 2 + 2 * 4 + 3 * 1 + 4 * 2)/(1 + 2 + 4 +

1 + 2) = 2.1. The median is the 50th percentile

value occurs at 2.

12. The probability will be the proportion of the area of the larger area to the total area. Draw x = 0, y = 0, x = 1, and y = 1; this forms a 1 by 1 square whose area equals 1. Draw the line y = -2x + 1 by recognizing its y-intercept is (0,1) and its x-intercept is (.5,0). Area 1 is the area bounded by x = 0, y = 0, and y = -2x + 1; this forms a right triangle whose area equals ½ base time height = ½ * 0.5 * 1.0 = ¼. The larger area, Area 2, equals the square minus the triangle, or 1 - ¼ = ¾. The probability equals (3/4)/1 = ¾.

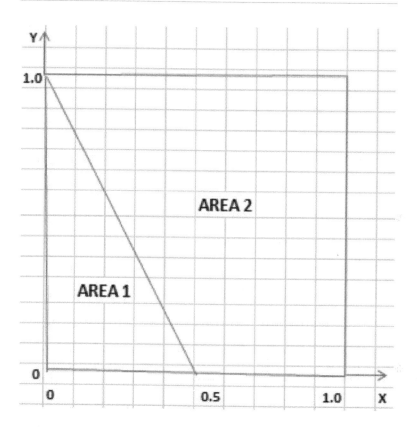

13. The sum of the probabilities equals 1.

   x + .05 + .30 + .05 + .20 + 2x + x = 1.

   4x + .60 = 1, 4x = .40, x = .10.

   Anteaters = .15, Elephants = .20, Ferrets = .10.

14. The Rodents have greater mean number of points per game than the Hamsters. The Rodents' data has a greater spread around its mean than the Hamsters does, and so a greater standard deviation.

15. D, whose points fit most closely to a straight line.

16. No. Correlation by itself cannot be used to conclude causation. There are other reasons that contribute to lung cancer such as environment, and this study has not isolated such other reasons.

Chapter 6

Sample Exam One

1. The height of a 5-year old child is approximately one:

   a. millimeter

   b. centimeter

   c. meter

   d. kilometer

   e. newton

2. How many whole numbers are there between - 2 and +2?

   a. 1

   b. 2

   c. 3

   d. 4

   e. 5

3. Which of the following expressions is equivalent to

   $(a^{-6})(b^{1/4})$?

   a. $(-a^6)(b^{1/4})$ d. $a^6/ \sqrt[4]{b}$

   b. $(ab)^{-3/2}$ e. $(\sqrt[4]{b})/ a^6$

   c. $a^6 \sqrt[4]{b}$

4. Multiply 6.2×10^3 by -3.1×10^{-6} and provide the

   answer in scientific notation.

   a. -19.22×10^{-3} d. -1.922×10^{-3}

   b. -19.22×10^3 e. -1.922×10^{-4}

   c. -1.922×10^{-2}

5. What is the least common multiple of 30 and 40?

   a. 10   d. 600

   b. 120   e. 1200

   c. 240

6. Between which two integers does $100^{1/3}$ fall?

    a. 0 and 1   d. 9 and 11

    b. 3 and 4   e. 33 and 34

    c. 4 and 5

7. Henry, Ina, and Jane read a total of 30 books. Ina read 80% of the number that Henry read, and Jane read 150% of the number that Ina read. How many did Henry read?

    a. 5   d. 12

    b. 8   e. 15

    c. 10

8. Calculate $\dfrac{\dfrac{-1}{3} + \dfrac{1}{4}}{\dfrac{1}{5}}$

    a. -5/12   d. -1/60

    b. -7/12   e. 7/60

    c. 7/12

9. School A and School B have the same ratio of boys to girls in their third grades. In school A, the ratio is 70:50. School B has 21 boys. How many girls does School B have?

   a. 12

   b. 15

   c. 18

   d. 20

   e. 28

10. How many prime numbers are there between 10 and 30?

   a. 4

   b. 5

   c. 6

   d. 7

   e. 8

11. 24 is 125% of what number?

   a. 12

   b. 15

   c. 18

   d. 19.2

   e. 30

12. An item costs $50 plus 8% sales tax. What will the cost be, including sales tax, after it goes on sale for 15% off?

a. $44.50

b. $44.90

c. $45.50

d. $45.90

e. $46.50

13. A job advertisement requires typing speed of 70 words per minute. At that speed, approximately how fast would the applicant type 300 words?

a. 4 minutes

b. 4 minutes and 10 seconds

c. 4 minutes and 20 seconds

d. 4 minutes and 30 seconds

e. 4 minutes and 40 seconds

14. A carpenter needs to cut a 3-foot long piece of wood into two parts whose lengths will be in a ratio of 5:7. How long will the parts be?

   a. 12 inches, 24 inches

   b. 13 inches, 23 inches

   c. 14 inches, 22 inches

   d. 15 inches, 21 inches

   e. 16 inches, 20 inches

15. A small Sicilian pizza is a 16-by-16-inch square and sells for $15. A large Sicilian pizza is a 28-by-16-inch rectangle. How much should the large pizza sell for if its price is to be fair relative to the small pizza?

   a. $24.50   d. $28.50

   b. $25.00   e. $30.00

   c. $26.25

16. A ball is dropped from a tall building. It is known that the distance y varies directly with the square of the time t the ball is falling. If the ball falls 64 feet in 2 seconds, how far will it fall in 8 seconds?

 a. 256 feet

 b. 512 feet

 c. 768 feet

 d. 1024 feet

 e. 2048 feet

17. Solve for x: $(x - 3)/(x + 3) = 9$

 a. -3.75

 b. -3

 c. 0

 d. 3

 e. 3.75

18. Solve for x: $3x - (15 - 4x) = 2x - (8 - 5x)$

 a. -3.5

 b. -3

 c. 3

 d. 3.5

 e. No solution

19. Simplify: $\dfrac{(2x+9)(5x-3)+(x^2+5)}{(2x+9)(x^3+5)}$

    a. $(x^2 + 5x + 2)/(x^3 + 5)$

    b. $(10x^2 + 5x + 2)/(x^3 + 5)$

    c. $(11x^2 + 39x - 22)/(11x^2 + 10x + 45)$

    d. $(10x^2 + 39x + 32)/(2x^4 + 9x^3 + 10x + 45)$

    e. $(11x^2 + 39x - 22)/(2x^4 + 9x^3 + 10x + 45)$

20. Simplify: $\dfrac{4x+3}{x^2-9} - \dfrac{x+1}{x-3}$

    a. $-x^2/(x^2 - 9)$

    b. $x^2/(x^2 - 9)$

    c. $(3x + 2)/(x^2 - 9)$

    d. $(-x^2 + 8x + 6)/(x^2 - 9)$

    e. $(x^2 + 8x + 6)/(x^2 - 9)$

21. Which of the following number lines on the graph (following) represents the solution to

$-5 \le 2x < 3$?

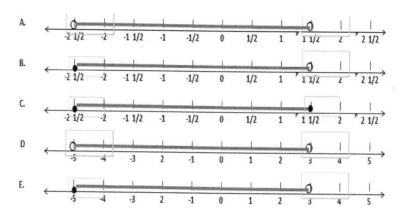

22. Find the slope of the straight line passing through the points (-1,-2) and (-5,-10).

a. -2

b. -1

c. 0

d. 1

e. 2

23. Find the equation of the straight line passing

through points (2,4) and (5,10).

   a. y =-2x + 4   d. y = 2x + 2

   b. y = -2x + 2   e. y = 2x + 4

   c. y = 2x

24. Let f(x) = $\dfrac{\sqrt{3x-6}}{(x-5)(x-2)}$. What is the domain of f?

   a. All real numbers x excluding x = 2 and x = 5

   b. All real numbers x > 2 excluding x = 5

   c. All real numbers x ≥ 2, excluding x = 5

   d. All real numbers, excluding x = 2 and x = 5

   e. All real numbers x

25. An elderly person with $100,000 to invest wants to

divide the $100,000 between a safe

investment earning 4% interest and a riskier

investment earning 8% interest, and she

wants the two investments to earn $5,500

interest in total. How much should she invest

in each investment?

a. $42,500 at 4%, and $57,500 at 8%.

b. $52,500 at 4%, and $47,500 at 8%.

c. $62,500 at 4%, and $37,500 at 8%.

d. $72,500 at 4%, and $27,500 at 8%.

e. $82,500 at 4%, and $17,500 at 8%.

26. Jan's salary is $44,000 less than twice Robin's salary, and their combined salary is $250,000. How much is Jan's salary?

   a. $ 98,000   d. $152,000

   b. $116,000   e. $170,000

   c. $134,000

27. Cell phone plan A costs $40 per month, plus 10 cents per minute. Plan B costs $45 per month, plus 25 cents per minute, in excess of 300 minutes. At approximately what number of minutes do the plans cost the same?

   a. 367   d. 500

   b. 400   e. 567

   c. 467

28. An inventor is selling his product for $800, and he

    has added 30% to his cost for his profit.

    Approximately what is his cost?

    a. $615   d. $660

    b. $630   e. $690

    c. $645

29. Roberta is buying fencing for her 288-square foot

    rectangular garden. The length is 2 times the

    width, and she only needs fencing for 3 sides

    because 1 of the 2 lengths is bordered by the

    house. How much fencing does she need?

    a. 48 feet   d. 144 feet

    b. 60 feet   e. 288 feet

    c. 72 feet

30. Solve for x: $|2 - 3x| < 13$.

    a. $x < 11/3$ d. $-5 < x < 11/3$

    b. $-11/3 < x < -5$ e. $-5 > x > 11/3$

    c. $11/3 < x < 5$

31. The equation of a circle with center at (0,0) and a radius of two is $x^2 + y^2 = 4$. If this is drawn on a xy-coordinate system, the vertical line test will demonstrate this is not a function. What if only the upper half of this circle was drawn. What is the domain D and the range R of this upper half circle?

    a. $D = \{-1 \le x \le +1\}$, $R = \{-1 \le y \le +1\}$

    b. $D = \{-2 \le x \le +2\}$, $R = \{0 \le y \le +2\}$

    c. $D = \{-2 \le x \le +2\}$, $R = \{-2 \le y \le +2\}$

    d. $D = \{$all real numbers $\ge 0\}$, $R = \{$all real numbers $\ge 0\}$

    e. $D = \{$all real numbers$\}$, $R = \{$all real numbers$\}$

32. Which of the four lines in the following figure

represents y = -2x + 2?

a. Line A

d. Line D

b. Line B

e. Line E

c. Line C

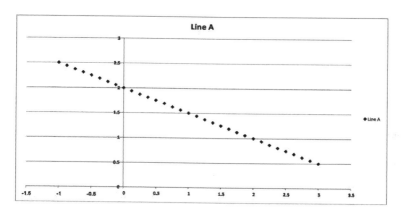

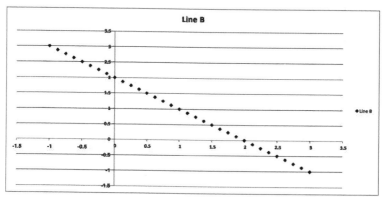

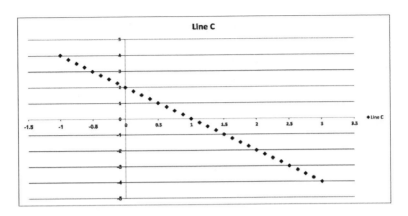

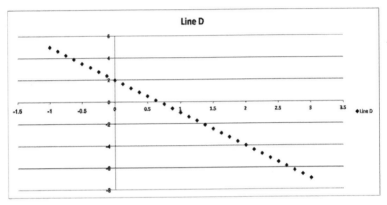

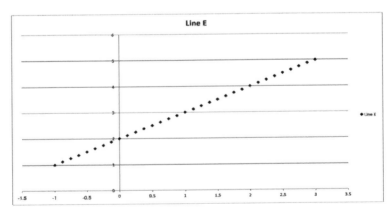

33. If the circular top of a cylinder has a circumference of 12π inches, and the cylinder has a volume of 108π cubic inches, what is the height of the cylinder?

a. 3 inches

b. 4.5 inches

c. 6 inches

d. 9 inches

e. 12 inches

34. The slow train from New York to Washington leaves at 9:00 a.m. The fast train from New York to Washington leaves at 10:00 a.m. and travels 30-mph faster than the slow train. How fast is each train traveling if the trains meet at an intermediate station at 11:30 a.m.?

a. 20 and 50 mph

b. 25 and 55 mph

c. 30 and 60 mph

d. 35 and 65 mph

e. 45 and 75 mph

35. If two angles are complementary such that one angle is 1/5th of the other, what are the measures of the angles?

a. 10° and 50°

b. 15° and 75°

c. 20° and 100°

d. 30° and 120°

e. 30° and 150°

36. In the diagram below, lines BC and ED are parallel, lines EF and GH are parallel, ∡ABC = 50°, and ∡DEF = 35°.

Calculate ∡FEG and ∡EGH.

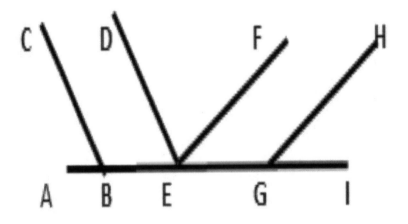

a. ∡FEG = 50° and ∡EGH = 130°

b. ∡FEG = 75° and ∡EGH = 85°

c. ∡FEG = 80° and ∡EGH = 100°

d. ∡FEG = 85° and ∡EGH = 95°

e. ∡FEG = 95° and ∡EGH = 85°

37. In the figure below, two concentric circles with

common center at O, have radii 1 and 2. The

larger circle is perfectly inscribed in square

ABCD such that the square touches the larger

circle only at points F, G, H, and I. J is a point

on the larger circle so that JOF forms a sector

of the circle, and ∡JOF = 45°.

What is the area of the region JEF?

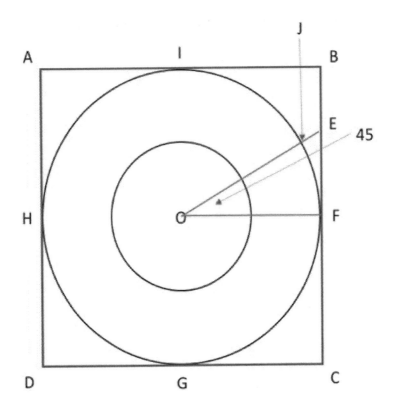

a. $2 - .5\pi$

d. $2 + 1.5\pi$

b. $2 + .5\pi$

e. $2 + 2\pi$

c. $2 - 1.5\pi$

38. Two sides of a triangle have lengths 4 and 8.

    What length can be third side be?

    a. 3

    b. 4

    c. 5

    d. 12

    e. 13

39. In the following diagram, Triangle I with vertices

    A, B, and C is drawn in the first quadrant.

    What are the coordinates of point B if the

    triangle is translated four units downward?

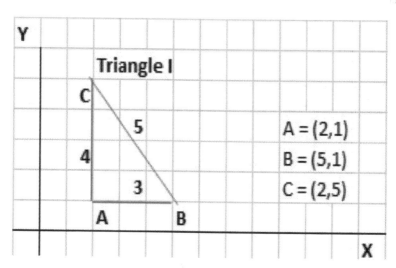

a. (1, 1)   d. (1, -5)

b. (5, 5)   e. (5, -1)

c. (5, -3)

40. Children build a snowman out of three spheres

with diameters of 30 inches for the head, 60

inches for the torso, and 90 inches for the

lower body. What is the total volume?

a. 4,200 π cubic inches

b. 16,800 π cubic inches

c. 162,000 π cubic inches

d. 486,000 π cubic inches

e. 1,296,000 π cubic inches

41. Let ABDEC be a polygon in the following

diagram. If a second polygon was drawn with

all sides three times the original polygon, what

would be the ratio of the area of the larger

polygon to the smaller polygon?

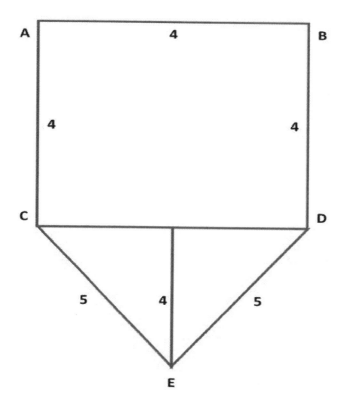

a. 2:1

b. 3:1

c. 5:1

d. 9:1

e. 22:1

42. Calculate the surface area of a rectangular solid
    having dimensions 8 inches by 10 inches by 2
    inches.

    a. 40 square inches

    b. 80 square inches

    c. 116 square inches

    d. 160 square inches

    e. 232 square inches

43. Calculate the area of the following figure:

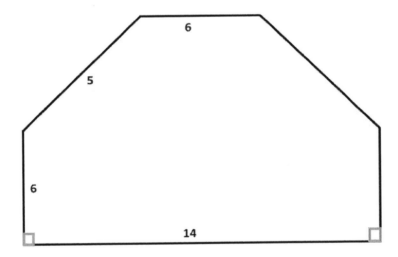

a. 42

d. 114

b. 87

e. 144

c. 107

44. Which of the following statements is FALSE?

a. A rectangle is a special kind of parallelogram.

b. If a quadrilateral has two pairs of sides of equal length, then the quadrilateral must be a parallelogram.

c. If a quadrilateral is a trapezoid, then there must be at least one pair of parallel opposite sides.

d. A quadrilateral always has the sum of its interior angles equal to 360°.

e. A quadrilateral always has each interior angle less than or equal to 180°.

45. Four of Mary's five test scores were 80, 85, 87, and 92. After her 5th test score, the mean value of all five scores was 87. What was her 5th test score?

  a. 87

  b. 88

  c. 89

  d. 90

  e. 91

46. A class of 9 students read the following numbers of books this year: 18, 21, 21, 23, 24, 25, 32, 35, and 38. The class calculated the resulting mean, median, mode, and range from those numbers. Then the class discovered the data value 38 was recorded incorrectly; the corrected value is 36. Which of the following calculations needs to be corrected?

a. Mean only

b. Mean and median only

c. Mean and mode only

d. Mean and range only

e. Mean, median, and range only

47. The following table shows numbers of signatures collected for a petition. If the data is graphed in a pie chart, what is the measure of the central angle for Beth's sector of the pie chart?

	Signatures
Arthur	24
Beth	18
Chris	12
Diane	6
Total	60

a. 18°

b. 30°

c. 60°

d. 72°

e. 108°

48. A six-sided die is created where the probability of each face is as follows. What is the probability of rolling a 4?

Face	1	2	3	4	5	6
Probability	x	2x	3x	4x	5x	6x

a. 1/6

b. 4/6

c. 1/7

d. 4/7

e. 4/21

49. A single playing card is drawn at random from a standard deck of 52 cards. What is the probability it is a diamond or a picture card?

a. 12/52

b. 16/52

c. 22/52

d. 25/52

e. 37/52

50. Which of the following CANNOT be calculated

from a boxplot?

a. mean

b. median

c. minimum data value

d. 25th percentile data value

e. range

51. Use the following stem-and-leaf plot to calculate

the mean of the data:

Stem	Leaf
3	5, 7
4	1, 1, 3, 4, 5
5	2, 5, 7

a. 42.5

b. 43

c. 43.5

d. 44

e. 45

52. The following graph displays the number of projects completed by each of 5 people. Calculate |mean - median|.

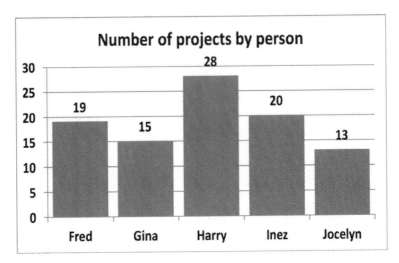

a. 0

b. 1

c. 2

d. 4

e. 9

53. The student council committee consists of 7 fifth-graders, 5 fourth-graders, and 8 third-graders. Each week 1 of these students is randomly selected to summarize the discussion to the principal, but the same student may not be selected more than once. What is the probability that a 5th-grader will be selected in 3 consecutive weeks? Round the final answer to three decimal places.

    a. .021

    b. .026

    c. .031

    d. .036

    e. .043

54. Sally and Ted are running for class president.

    Students vote by raising their hands; 47

    students raised their hands to vote for Sally;

    48 students raised their hands to vote for Ted;

    24 students voted for both candidates. It was

    decided not to count the 24 votes for both

    candidates. Who won and by how much?

    a. Sally won by 2 votes

    b. Sally won by 1 vote

    c. Ted won by 2 votes

    d. Ted won by 1 vote

    e. Sally and Ted received the same number

55. When 2 dice are rolled, what is the probability

    their sum will be 5?

    a. 2/36   d. 5/36

    b. 3/36   e. 6/36

    c. 4/36

56. Use the following box plot to calculate the
    difference between the range and the
    interquartile range.

    a. 30   d. 60

    b. 40   e. 100

    c. 50

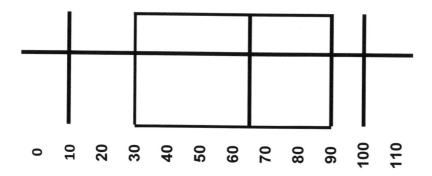

Chapter 7

Answers to Sample Exam One

1. Answer: c. You should know 10 mm = 1 cm, 100 cm = 1 m, 1 km = 1,000 m. Also, 1 inch = 2.54 cm, 1 m ≈ 1 yard, 1 km ≈ .62 miles. A 5-year old child is approximately 3-feet tall or 1-meter.

2. Answer: b. The whole numbers are the natural numbers plus 0. The word 'between' in this question suggests not to count the ending value of +2; 0 and 1 are the whole numbers between -2 and +2.

3. Answer: e. $(a^{-6}) = 1/a^6$. $b^{1/4} = \sqrt[4]{b}$. $(a^{-6})(b^{1/4}) = (\sqrt[4]{b})/a^6$.

4. Answer: c. 6.2×10^3 by $-3.1 \times 10^{-6} = (-6.2 * 3.1) *$

$(10^3 * 10^{-6}) = -19.22 * 10^{-3} = (-19.22/10)*(10^{-3} *$

$10) = -1.922 \times 10^{-2}$. Note that a is an

equivalent answer, but it is not in scientific

notation.

5. Answer: b. Multiples of 30: 30, 60, 90, 120, ...

Multiples of 40: 40, 80, 120, ... Answer: 120.

6. Answer: c. You need to recognize $100^{1/3} = \sqrt[3]{100}$,

which asks for what x does $x^3 = 100$? By trial

and error, $4^3 = 64$ and $5^3 = 125$. So, $4 < 100^{1/3}$

< 5.

7. Answer: c. Let x = number of books Henry read,

.80x = number of books Ina read, and

$1.50(.80x) = 1.2x$ = number of books Jane

read. $x + .80x + 1.2x = 30$, $3x = 30$, $x = 10$.

8. Answer: a. $\dfrac{\frac{-1}{3}+\frac{1}{4}}{\frac{1}{5}}$ = ((-1/3) * (4/4) + (1/4) *

(3/3)) / (1/5) = ((-4 + 3)/12)/(1/5) = (-1/12)/(1/5)

= (-1/12)(5/1) = -5/12.

9. Answer: b. Let x = number of girls in School B.

70/50 = 21/x; x(70/50) = x(21/x);

x(70/50)(50/70) = 21(50/70); x = 3 * 50/10 = 15.

10. Answer: c. {11,13,17,19,23,29}.

11. Answer: d. 24 = 1.25x, x = 24/1.25 = 19.2

12. Answer: d. The amount of the discount is

.15 * 50 = $7.50, the discounted price is

50 - 7.50 = $42.50, the sales tax alone is

$42.50 * .08 = $3.40, so the total price is

$42.50 + $3.40 = $45.90. The quicker solution

is 50 * .85 * 1.08 = $45.90.

13. Answer: c. This is a ratio problem. 70 words / 1 minute = 300 words / x minutes. x = 300 words / (70 words / minute) = 4.29 minutes. But the answer choices are in seconds, and .29 minutes ≠ 29 seconds. .29 minutes = .29 minutes*(60 seconds/1 minute) = 17.4 seconds. The closest answer is c.

14. Answer: d. Let x = constant of proportionality. 5x + 7x = 3. 12x = 3, x = 3/12 = .25 feet. 5 * .25 = 1.25 feet, 7 *.25 = 1.75 feet. The answer choices are in inches; 1.25 feet * 12 inches / 1 foot = 15 inches, 1.75 ft. = 21 in.

15. Answer: c. Unit price is price per unit of measure, and the measure is area. The area of the small is 16 * 16 = 256 square inches, and the area of the large is 28 * 16 = 448 square inches. Let x = price of large. 15/256 = x/448, x = $26.25.

16. Answer: d. Let y = distance in eight seconds.

    $64/2^2 = y/8^2$, y = 64 * 64/4 = 1024

17. Answer: a. (x-3)/(x+3) =9; x - 3 = (x + 3) * 9,

    x - 3 = 9x + 27, 8x = -30, x = -3.75

18. Answer: e. Left side: 3x - (15 - 4x) = 2x - (8 -

    5x) = 3x -15 + 4x = 7x - 15. Right side:

    2x - 8 + 5x = 7x - 8, so we have

    7x -15 = 7x -8, 0 x = 7. There is NO solution!

19. Answer: e. Numerator is (2x + 9)(5x - 3) +

    $(x^2 + 5) = (10x^2 + 39x - 27) + (x^2 + 5) = 11x^2 +$

    39x - 22. Denominator is $2x^4 + 9x^3 + 10x + 45$.

20. Answer: a. $(4x + 3)/(x^2 - 9) - (x + 1)/(x - 3) =$

    $(4x + 3)/(x^2 - 9) - (x + 1)/(x - 3) * (x + 3)/(x + 3)$

    $= ((4x + 3) - (x^2 + 4x + 3))/(x^2 - 9) = -x^2/(x^2 - 9)$.

21. Answer: b. $-5 \le 2x < 3$. $-5/2 \le 2x/2 < 3/2$, $-2.5 \le x$

    < 1.5

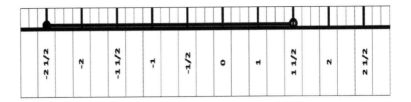

22. Answer: e. Let $(x_1, y_1) = (-1, -2)$ and $(x_2, y_2) =$

    $(-5, -10)$. Then $m = (y_2 - y_1)/(x_2 - x_1) =$

    $(-10 - - 2)/(-5 - - 1) = -8/-4 = +2$.

23. Answer: c. Calculate

    $m = (10 - 4)/(5 - 2) = 6/3 = 2$.

    Choose $(2,4)$, and plug into $y - y_1 = m(x - x_1)$:

    $y - 4 = 2(x - 2)$, $y - 4 = 2x - 4$, $y = 2x$.

24. Answer: b. $\dfrac{\sqrt{3x - 6}}{(x - 5)(x - 2)}$ The numerator cannot

    be negative, so $3x - 6 \ge 0$, $x \ge 2$. The

    denominator cannot be zero, so exclude $x = 2$

    and $x = 5$.

25. Answer: c. Let x = amount invested at 4%, and

$100,000 - x = amount invested at 8%. Then

.04x + .08(100000 - x) = $5,500; .04x + $8,000

-.08x = $5,500; -.04x + $8,000 = $5,500; .04x =

2500, x = $62,500; $100,000 - x = $37,500.

Check: .04 * $62,500 + .08 * $37,500 =

$5,500.

26. Answer: d. Let x = Robin's salary and 2x -

$44,000 = Jan's salary. Then x + 2x - $44,000

= $250,000; 3x = $294,000; x = $98,000;

2 * $98,000 - $44,000 = $152,000.

27. Answer: c. Let x = number of minutes when

plans cost the same.

40 + .10x = 45 + .25(x - 300).

Then 40 + .10x = 45 + .25x - 75, 40 +.10x =

.25x-30, 70 = .15x, x = 466.7.

28. Answer: a. Let x = his cost. Then x + .30x =

800; 1.30x = 800; x = 800/1.3 = 615.38

29. Answer: a. Let x = width, and 2x = length.

    Area = length * width = (x)(2x) = 288.

    $2x^2 = 288$, $x^2 = 144$, x = 12, 2x = 24.

    The amount of fencing is 2 widths plus 1

    length: 2 * 12 + 1 * 24 = 48.

30. Answer: c. This is equivalent to

    -13 < 2 - 3x < +13.

    Add -2 to all three terms, so -15 < -3x < 11.

    Divide -3 by all three terms and change the

    direction of the inequality, so 15/3 > x > -11/3.

    This is equivalent to -11/3 < x < +5.

31. Answer: b. See the following graph:

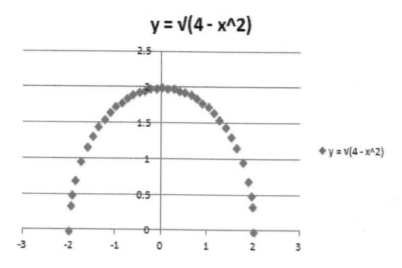

$$y = \sqrt{(4 - x^{\wedge}2)}$$

32. Answer: c. y = -2x + 2 has y-intercept 2 and

slope - 2. All five curves pass through (0,2), so

they all have y-intercept 2. A slope of -2 says

for each increase of x by 1, y will change by -2.

Note that from (0,2) to (1,0) the slope will be -2.

Only line C passes through (1,0).

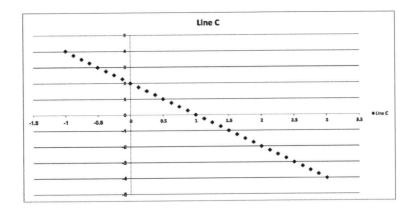

33. Answer: a. Circumference of top = $12\pi = 2\pi r$, so

r= 6. Volume of cylinder = $108\pi = \pi r^2 h = \pi 6^2 h$

= $36\pi h$, h = $108\pi/36\pi$ = 3.

34. Answer: e. Let x = speed of slow train, and

x + 30 = speed of fast train. At 11:30 they

have traveled a Distance equaling Rate * Time

of 2.5x and 1.5(x + 30) respectively. They

have traveled the same distance, so 2.5x =

1.5(x + 30); 2.5x = 1.5x + 45; x = 45;

x + 30 = 75.

35. Answer: b. Let x = smaller angle, and 5x = larger angle. x + 5x = 90; 6x = 90; x = 15°; 5x = 75°.

36. Answer: e. Lines BC and ED are parallel, so ∡ABC and ∡BED are corresponding angles and each equals 50°. ∡BED, ∡DEF, and ∡FEG are supplementary, so ∡FEG = 180 - 50 - 35 = 95. Lines EF and GH are parallel, so ∡FEG and ∡HGI are corresponding angles and each equals 95°. ∡EGH and ∡HGI are supplementary, so ∡EGH = 180 - 95 = 85. So ∡FEG = 95°, and ∡EGH = 85°.

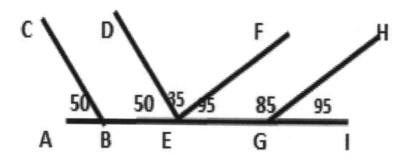

37. Answer: a. The area of region JEF equals the area of △ OFE minus the area of sector JOF in the following diagram. The square touching the larger circle only at point F says that line BFC is a tangent line to the circle, so ∡OFE = 90°. So △OFE is a right triangle.

∡JOF = 45°, so ∡OEF must also equal 45°, and △ OFE is an isosceles right triangle. Line OF is a radius that equals 2, so line EF must also equal 2. The area of △ OFE equals (1/2)(base)(height) = (1/2)(2)(2) = 2. The area of the larger circle equals $\pi r^2 = \pi 2^2 = 4\pi$. The area of sector JOF = (45/360)(4π) = (1/8) (4π) = .5π. The area of region JEF equals 2 - .5π.

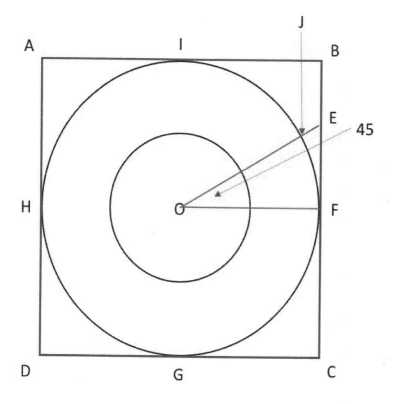

38. Answer: c. The Triangle Inequality says the sum of any two sides of a triangle must be greater than the third side; 4 + 8 = 12, so 12 or 13 cannot be the third side; 3 cannot be the third side because 3 + 4 is not greater than 8; and 4 cannot be the third side because 4 + 4 is not greater than 8; 5 can be the third side because 5 + 4 > 8, 5 + 8 > 4, and 4 + 8 > 5.

39. Answer: c. Point B is (5,1). If it is translated down it becomes (5,-3).

40. Answer: c. Volume of a sphere = $(4/3)\pi r^3$. The given data is for diameters.

$(4/3) \pi\ 15^3 + (4/3) \pi\ 30^3 + (4/3) \pi\ 45^3 = (4/3) \pi(15^3 + 30^3 + 45^3) = (4/3) \pi(121,500) = 162,000\pi$ cubic inches.

41. Answer: d. If the sides are multiplied by 3, then the area is multiplied by $3^2 = 9$. The answer is 9:1. It is not necessary to calculate areas, but if you do, the area of the smaller is $4^2 + (1/2)(5)(4) = 26$, the area of the larger is $12^2 + (1/2)(15)(12) = 234$, which is 9:1.

42. Answer: e. There are 6 rectangular sides: 2 sides that are 8 * 10, 2 sides that are 8 * 2, and two sides that are 10 * 2. The surface area is 2*(8 * 10 + 8 * 2 + 10 * 2) = 232 square inches.

43. Answer: d. Draw additional lines as shown below. The figure is a trapezoid with area $(1/2)(height)(base_1 + base_2)$, plus a rectangle with area (length)(width). The height h of the trapezoid is not given, but by the Pythagorean Theorem it equals $h = \sqrt{(5^2 - 4^2)} = 3$.

So area of trapezoid is (1/2)(3)(6 + 14), or 30.

Area of rectangle is 6 * 14 = 84.

Total area is 30 + 84 = 114.

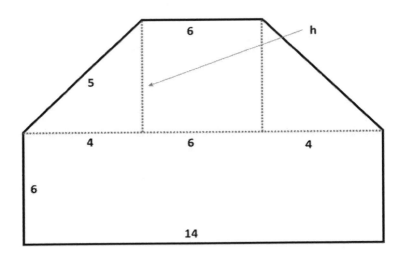

44. Answer: b. A kite has 2 pairs of equal sides that are adjacent to each other.

45. Answer: e. Let x = the fifth test score. Then

(80 + 85 + 87 + 92 + x)/5 = 87.

So (344 + x)/5 = 87; 344 + x = 87*5;

344 + x = 435; x = 435 - 344 = 91.

46. Answer: d. The mean is calculated using every number. The median was and is 24. The mode was and is 21. The range equals maximum value minus minimum value, and the maximum has changed.

47. Answer: e. Beth's signatures are 18/60 or 30% of the total. The central angle of the pie chart will be 30% of 360^0, or, 108^0.

48. Answer: e. The sum of all possible probabilities equals 1. So, $x + 2x + 3x + 4x + 5x + 6x = 1$. $21x = 1$; $x = 1/21$; $4x = 4/21$.

49. Answer: c. The probability of a diamond is 13/52. The probability of a picture card is 12/52. The probability of a diamond picture card is 3/52. The answer is $13/52 + 12/52 - 3/52 = 22/52$.

50. Answer: a. The remaining choices can be calculated from a box-plot.

51. Answer: e. (35 + 37 + 41 + 41 + 43 + 44 + 45 + 52 + 55 + 57)/10 = 45.

52. Answer: a. The mean equals

(19 + 15 + 28 + 20 +13)/5 = 95/5 = 19.

The median is the middle number, when sorted from low to high, which is 19. |19 - 19| = 0.

53. Answer: c. There are 7 + 5 + 8 = 20 students.

The probability is (7/20)(6/19)(5/18) = 210/6840 = .0307 or .031 (rounded).

54. Answer: d. Draw a Venn Diagram as shown below.

Votes for Sally and Ted

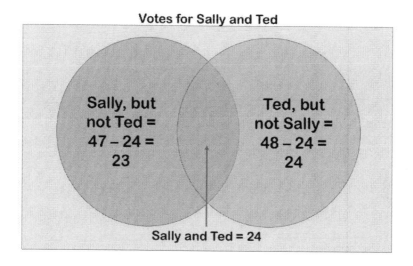

55. Answer: c. There are 6 * 6 = 36 outcomes from rolling two dice. There are 4 ways to get a sum of 5: {(1,4), (2,3), (3,2), (4,1)}. The probability is 4/36.

56. Answer: a. Range = maximum - minimum = 100 - 10 = 90. Interquartile range = 90 - 30 = 60; 90 - 60 = 30.

Chapter 8

Sample Exam Two

1. The bill for dinner is $50.00, including 7% tax. You realize you forgot to give the waiter a coupon for 15% discount before tax and you do so. You want to give a 20% tip on the undiscounted amount, before tax. What is the final cost of the dinner? (Round each calculation to the nearest penny.)

   a. $51.00

   b. $51.85

   c. $52.50

   d. $54.15

   e. $60.00

2. Which of the following is the most likely height of a

   dining room table?

   a. 100 millimeters

   b. 10 centimeters

   c. 1 decimeter

   d. 1 meter

   e. .01 kilometer

3. Which of the following is NOT an irrational

   number?

   a. $(\sqrt{3})/3$ d. $(\sqrt{6})/(\sqrt{3})$

   b. $(\sqrt[3]{3})/3$ e. $(\sqrt{27})/(\sqrt{3})$

   c. $\pi/3$

4. Calculate: 5 - 6(5 - 8)/9 * 10

   a. -15   d. 170/90

   b. 10/9   e. 25

   c. 468/90

5. Find the Greatest Common Factor of 144 and 160.

   a. 8   d. 64

   b. 16   e. 1440

   c. 32

6. You bought a share of stock 10 years ago for $10. It has increased in value by 250%. What is its new value?

   a. $12.50   d. $30.00

   b. $15.00   e. $35.00

   c. $25.00

7. Calculate $-\dfrac{1}{4}+1\dfrac{2}{5}-\dfrac{2}{3}$

   a. .48   d. 109/60

   b. .17/30   e. 135/60

   c. 29/60

8. Calculate $9^{-1/2}$.

    a. -4.5

    b. -1/3

    c. 1/3

    d. 18

    e. 81

9. A professional sports team signed three new players with signing bonuses in the ratio of 6:4:2. The second largest bonus was $1,600,000. What is the total of the three bonuses?

    a. $2,400,000

    b. $3,600,000

    c. $4,800,000

    d. $5,400,000

    e. $6,000,000

10. Multiply -5.1 X 10^{-2} by 3.9 X 10^4 and provide the answer in scientific notation.

    a. -19.89 X 10^{-8}

    b. -19.89 X 10^2

    c. -1.989 X 10^{-7}

    d. -1.989 X 10^2

    e. -1.989 X 10^3

11. 48 is 12.5% of what number?

    a. 6   d. 384

    b. 38.4   e. 400

    c. 54.9

12. Calculate $\sqrt{600} - \sqrt{150}$

    a. $5\sqrt{3}$ d. $3\sqrt{10}$

    b. $6\sqrt{5}$ e. $\sqrt{450}$

    c. $5\sqrt{6}$

13. Calculate $\dfrac{x-y}{-z+w}$ if x = 1; y = -1; z = 1; w = -1.

    a. -2   d. 1

    b. -1   e. 2

    c. 0

14. What number is in the tenths place if 1.234567 x 10^5 is multiplied by 10^{-2}?

    a. 2   d. 5

    b. 3   e. 6

    c. 4

15. Which expression best represents the following data:

x	y
1	3
2	5
3	7
4	9
5	11

a. $y = -x + 4$

b. $y = x + 2$

c. $y = 2x + 1$

d. $y = x^2 + 2$

e. $y = x^3 + 2$

16. One website says to cook a 20-pound turkey for 4 and 2/3 hours. If cooking time is proportional to weight, approximately how long should you cook a 14-pound turkey?

a. 3 hours, 5 minutes

b. 3 hours, 16 minutes

c. 3 hours, 27 minutes

d. 3 hours, 38 minutes

e. 4 hours

17. Perform the indicated operations, and write the answer in simplest expression:

$(9x^2 + 8x - 6) - (2x^2 - 5x) - (-5x^3 - 3x^2 + 4)$.

    a. $-5x^3 + 14x^2 + 13x - 10$

    b. $5x^3 + 10x^2 + 3x + 10$

    c. $5x^3 + 14x^2 + 13x - 10$

    d. $5x^3 + 10x^2 + 3x - 2$

    e. $5x^3 + 10x^2 + 13x - 10$

18. Perform the indicated operations, and write the answer in simplest expression: $(x^3 + 2)(x^2 - 1)$.

    a. $x^5 + x^3 - 2x^2 - 2$

    b. $x^6 - x^3 + 2x^2 - 2$

    c. $x^5 + 2x^3 - 2x^2 - 2$

    d. $x^5 - x^3 + 2x^2 - 2$

    e. $x^6 - x^3 + 2x^2 - 2$

19. The formula to convert Celsius temperature C into Fahrenheit temperature F is

    F = (9/5)C + 32. Use that formula to convert Fahrenheit temperature F into Celsius temperature C.

    a. C = 5*(F - 32)

    b. C = F - 32*(5/9)

    c. C = F + 32*(5/9)

    d. C = (5/9) (F - 32)

    e. C = (5/9) (F + 32)

20. Five years ago Lou was 4 times as old as Betty was then; 15 years from now, Lou will be twice as old as Betty will be then. How old is Lou now?

    a. 20

    b. 28

    c. 30

    d. 45

    e. 60

21. A product costs some number of dollars to make. The sales price of $490.00 is determined by adding an additional 22.5% of that cost. Calculate the cost to make the product.

    a. $380.00

    b. $390.00

    c. $400.00

    d. $410.00

    e. $420.00

22. Find the value of x such that the slope of the line through the points (6,17) and (x,5) will equal 3.

    a. -30   d. 2

    b. -2   e. 30

    c. 1

23. Find the equation of the straight line passing

through the points (1,7) and (2,10).

a. -6x + y = 4

b. -6x + 2y = 4

c. -6x + y = 8

d. -6x + 2y = 8

e. y = 3x + 2

24. What is the equation of the line shown in the

following diagram?

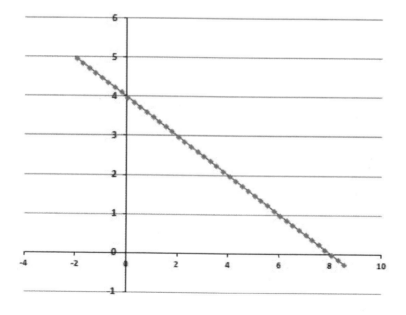

a. $y = -.5x + 4$

b. $y = -.5x + 8$

c. $y = -x + 4$

d. $y = -x + 8$

e. $y = -2x + 4$

25. Find 3 consecutive odd numbers whose sum is 171.

a. 56, 57, 58

b. 51, 53, 55

c. 53, 55, 57

d. 55, 57, 59

e. 57, 59, 61

26. A 2-digit number has the property that its ten's digit is 2 times its unit's digit. When the digits are reversed, the reversed number is 27 less than the original number. What is the original number?

a. 21

b. 24

c. 42

d. 63

e. 84

27. Flo counted the coins in a jar and counted $13.00 in nickels, dimes, and quarters. She had twice as many dimes as quarters, and she had twice as many nickels as dimes. How many dimes did she have?

a. 10

b. 20

c. 30

d. 40

e. 50

28. A movie theatre sold 200 tickets. Some customers paid the regular price of $12.00 per ticket, and some customers had a coupon entitling them to a 25% discount. The total sales were $2,250. What percent of customers had the coupon?

    a. 10%

    b. 20%

    c. 25%

    d. 30%

    e. 50%

29. Harry and Larry start walking towards each other from opposite ends of Main Street. At the start, they are 1.4 miles apart. Harry walks at a constant 3 miles per hour, and Larry walks at a constant 4 miles per hour. How far will Harry have walked when they meet?

a. .35 miles

d. .50 miles

b. .40 miles

e. .60 miles

c. .45 miles

30. A juice manufacturer wants to mix some quantity of a 33% juice with another quantity of a 28% juice to create 20 ounces of a 30% juice. What quantity of the 33% juice should he use?

a. 6 ounces

d. 9 ounces

b. 7 ounces

e. 10 ounces

c. 8 ounces

31. Ann can do a job in 3 hours. Bob can do the same job in 2 hours. Carol can do the same job in 4 hours. How long would it take them to do the job if they worked together?

a. $1/9$ hours

d. 1 hour

b. ½ hour

e. $13/12$ hours

c. $12/13$ hours

32. Tynice invested an amount of money into a fund earning 6.5% interest, and an amount that was $2,000 greater into a fund earning 8.0% interest. The total interest earned was $305.00. How much did she invest in the 6.5% account?

a. $1,000

b. $1,500

c. $2,000

d. $2,500

e. $3,000

33. The lengths of a scalene triangle are consecutive even integers. The perimeter equals 8 more than 2 times the largest side. How long is the largest side?

a. 8

b. 10

c. 12

d. 14

e. 16

34. In the diagram below, given that Lines 1 and 2 are parallel, find the measure of angle y.

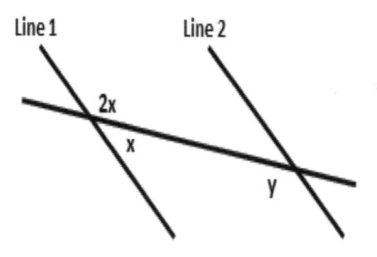

a. 30°

b. 60°

c. 110°

d. 120°

e. There is not enough information to answer this problem.

35. In the following diagram, line DE is parallel to line BC. What is the value of y?

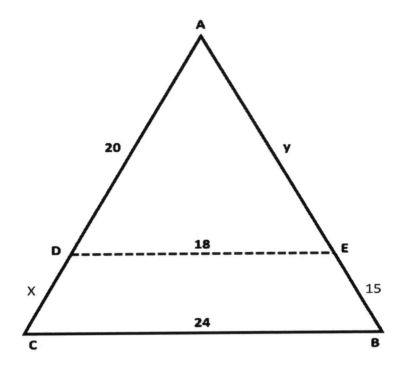

a. 25

b. 30

c. 35

d. 40

e. 45

36. Let ABCD be a parallelogram with AB = 3x + 4,

   AC = 5x + 2, perimeter = 44, and area = 60.

   Calculate the height AE for the following

   diagram.

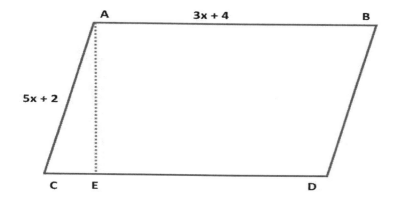

a. 5

b. 6

c. 8

d. 10

e. 12

37. A circle with a diameter of two inches has a 45°
central angle. Approximately what is the
measure of the arc formed by that angle?

    a. .25 inches

    b. .395 inches

    c. .785 inches

    d. 1.258 inches

    e. 1.57 inches

38. If the volume of a cube is 125 cubic feet, find its
surface area.

    a. 50 square feet

    b. 75 square feet

    c. 100 square feet

    d. 125 square feet

    e. 150 square feet

39. The following diagram shows a prism whose base is a right triangle with sides a, b, and c. If the volume is 60 cubic feet, the hypotenuse c is 5 feet, and b is 4 feet, calculate the height.

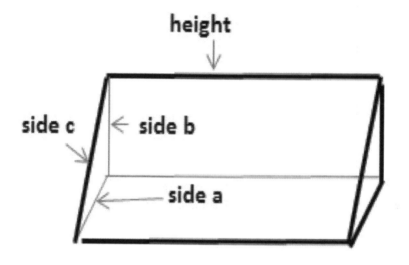

a. 8 feet

b. 10 feet

c. 12 feet

d. 16 feet

e. 18 feet

40. In the diagram below, which triangle represents the result after Triangle I is rotated 180 degrees about the origin?

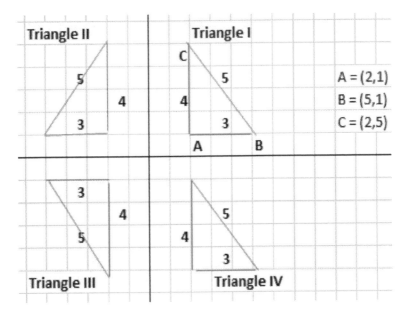

a. Triangle I

b. Triangle II

c. Triangle III

d. Triangle IV

e. None of the above.

41. Suppose with two concentric circles the circumference of the larger circle is twice as large as the circumference of the smaller circle. What is the ratio of the area in between the circles to the area of the smaller circle?

a. 1:1

b. 2:1

c. 3:1

d. 4:1

e. 4π:1

42. A cylindrical-shaped can of paint fits perfectly in a cube-shaped box. Approximately what percent of the box is not used by the can?

a. 10.5%

b. 13.5%

c. 17.0%

d. 21.5%

e. 25%

43. The following diagram shows a cone with height 20 and diameter 10. Suppose the bottom of the cone, which has a height of 8 and a diameter of 4, is cut off at AB, leaving the upper portion (called a conical frustrum). What is the volume of this upper portion?

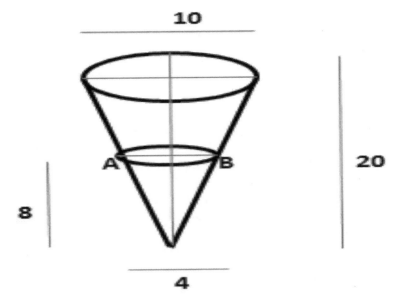

a. $(234/3)\pi$

b. 234π

c. $(468/3)\pi$

d. 468π

e. $(1872/3)\pi$

44. In a standard deck of cards with the seven of hearts missing, if one card is randomly selected what is the probability of randomly selecting a diamond or a heart?

a. 24/51

d. 25/52

b. 25/51

e. 26/52

c. 26/51

45. The following table displays 100 people who were asked how many movies they watched last month. If a person is chosen at random from those who saw one or more movies, what is the probability that person is an Easterner?

	None	1 to 3	4 or More	Total
Westerners	25	15	10	50
Easterners	30	15	5	50
Total	55	30	15	100

a. $^{15}/_{30}$ d. $^{20}/_{100}$

b. $^{20}/_{30}$ e. $^{50}/_{100}$

c. $^{20}/_{45}$

46. The ace of hearts, the king of hearts, and the queen of hearts are placed in a bowl. A card is randomly selected, and then returned to the bowl. Then a second card is randomly selected. What is the probability that the ace was never selected?

a. $^{2}/_{9}$ d. $^{5}/_{9}$

b. $^{3}/_{9}$ e. $^{6}/_{9}$

c. $^{4}/_{9}$

47. A basketball player has a 60% probability of successfully making a free throw. If she is successful, she is given a second opportunity to make another free throw. Her probability of success is constant each time she tries. What is the probability distribution for her number of successful free throws?

a. $P(0) = 40\%$, $P(1) = 60\%$.

b. $P(0) = 40\%$, $P(1) = 24\%$, $P(2) = 36\%$.

c. $P(0) = 40\%$, $P(1) = 30\%$, $P(2) = 30\%$.

d. $P(0) = 60\%$, $P(1) = 40\%$.

e. $P(0) = 60\%$, $P(1) = 20\%$, $P(2) = 20\%$.

48. Use the following boxplot to calculate the difference between the range and the median.

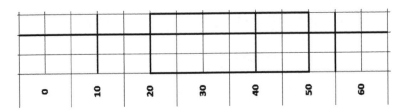

a. 5

b. 10

c. 15

d. 20

e. 25

49. The following table is the result of a survey of how many lipsticks that women carry in their bag. Calculate the mean, median, and mode.

Number of Lipsticks Carried	Probability
0	20%
1	25%
2	25%
3	20%
4	10%

a. Mean = 1.75. It is not possible to calculate median or mode.

b. Mean = 1.75. Median = 2. Mode = 2.

c. Mean = 1.75. Median = 2. Mode = 1 and 2.

d. Mean = 2. It is not possible to calculate median or mode.

e. Mean = 2. Median = 2. Mode = 1 and 2.

50. Which of the following CANNOT be calculated from a stem-and-leaf diagram?

    a. mean

    b. median

    c. minimum data value

    d. 25th percentile data value

    e. None of the above.

51. The table below shows the results when 300 people were asked to name their favorite sports team. According to the table, which of the following statements is NOT true:

Sports Team	Fans
Anteaters	15%
Beavers	25%
Chipmunks	30%
Deer	20%
Eels	10%

a. The number who chose Beavers is 30 more than the number who chose Anteaters.

b. The number who chose Chipmunks is 15 more than the number who chose Beavers.

c. The number who chose Anteaters plus the number who chose Eels is 15 more than the number who chose Deer.

d. The number who chose Chipmunks is 25 more than the number who chose Deer.

e. The number who chose Eels is 45 less than the number who chose Beavers.

52. Suppose the majority of the children's weights are between 40 and 50 pounds, but it was discovered the scale malfunctioned, and everyone's weight was understated by 4 pounds. When the data is adjusted by these 4

pounds, which of the following is NOT true.

a. The mean weight will increase by 4 pounds.

b. The median weight will increase by 4 pounds.

c. The mode weight will increase by 4 pounds.

d. The range will increase by 4 pounds.

e. The standard deviation will increase by 4 pounds.

53. A scatterplot is drawn comparing number of hours studied versus Praxis exam grade. Which of the following is true?

a. A high positive correlation exists when the points show a positive slope and are a distance from the best fitting straight line.
b. A high positive correlation exists when the points show a nearly vertical slope.
c. A high positive correlation exists when the points show a nearly horizontal slope.
d. Correlation is not affected by which variable is called x and which is called y.
e. A strong positive correlation says we can conclude that greater number of hours studied causes a higher exam grade.

54. A hotel is experimenting with its room prices with the following results (see table below). How much more income did the hotel receive at the $200.00 price compared with the $100.00 price?

Daily Room Price	Number of Rooms Rented
$100.00	120
$150.00	95
$200.00	65

a. $10,000.00

b. $22,500.00

c. $35,000.00

d. $42,000.00

e. $47,500.00

55. The following diagram represents students who are taking A=algebra, B=biology, and C=chemistry. There are four overlapping regions labeled 1, 2, 3, and 4. What does region 1 plus 4 represent?

Students taking Algebra, Biology, Chemistry

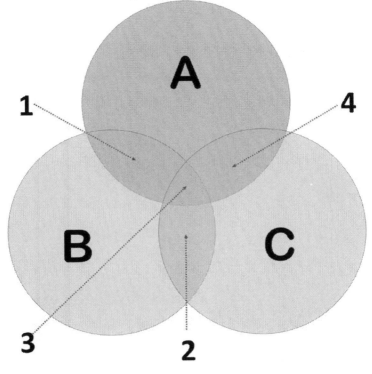

a. Students taking algebra, biology, and chemistry

b. Students taking algebra and biology, but not chemistry.

c. Students taking algebra and biology, or algebra and chemistry.

d. Students taking algebra and chemistry, but not biology.

e. Students taking algebra and biology, or biology and chemistry.

56. Five-hundred voters voted for exactly one of Candidate A, B, C, or D, but a mechanical failure in the voting booth prevented the votes for Candidates B and D from being recorded. What is the largest number of votes that Candidate D could have received?

	Voters
Candidate A	275
Candidate B	unknown
Candidate C	85
Candidate D	unknown

a. 69

b. 70

c. 139

d. 140

e. 500

Chapter 9

Answers to Sample Exam Two

1. Answer: a. Let x = the bill before discount and

   tax. Then the tax is .07x, and x + .07x =

   $50.00. So, 1.07x = 50, x = 50/1.07 = $46.73

   rounded. A 15% discount on $46.73 is

   .15 * $46.73 = $7.01 rounded; the discounted

   bill before tax is $46.73 - $7.01 = $39.72;

   7% tax on $39.72 is .07 * $39.72 = 2.78; a 20%

   tip on the undiscounted $46.73 is .20 * $46.73

   = $9.35. The final cost is $39.72 + $2.78 +

   $9.35 = $51.85.

2. Answer: d. The height is about 3 feet, which is close to 1 meter. 1 cm. ~ 0.4 inches, 10 cm. = 100 mm = 1 dm. ~ 4 inches. 1 km. ~ .6 mile = .6*5280 ft. = 3168 ft., .01 km ~ 32 ft.

3. Answer: e. $(\sqrt{27})/(\sqrt{3}) = \sqrt{(27/3)} = \sqrt{9} = 3 = {}^3/_1$.

4. Answer: e. $5 - 6(5 - 8)/9 * 10 = 5 - 6(-3)/9 * 10 = 5 + 18/9 * 10 = 5 + 2 * 10 = 25$.

5. Answer: b. Write out the prime factors of each and look for the largest common factor. $144 = 12 * 12 = 4 * 3 * 4 * 3 = 2 * 2 * 2 * 2 * 3 * 3 = 2^4 * 3^2$; $160 = 16 * 10 = 4 * 4 * 5 * 2 = 2^5 * 5$. So, $2^4 = 16$ is the largest common factor.

6. Answer: e. If something increases by x%, its New value equals Old Value * (1 + x%). 10 * (1 + 250%) = 10 * (1 + 2.5) = 10 * 3.5 = 35. Another way to think about this problem is, if the $10 stock increased 100%, then the new value is $20; if instead the $10 stock increased 200%, then its new value is $30; and if instead the $10 stock increased 300%, then its new value is $40. The 250% is halfway between 30 and 40.

7. Answer: c. The lowest common denominator is 60, so convert each term to 60ths. Note that $1\frac{2}{5}$ equals $^7/_5$. Multiply the three terms by $^{15}/_{15}$, $^{12}/_{12}$, and $^{20}/_{20}$ respectively. $-\frac{1}{4} + 1\frac{2}{5} - \frac{2}{3}$

equals $-\frac{15}{60} + \frac{84}{60} - \frac{40}{60}$, or $^{29}/_{60}$.

8. Answer: c. A negative exponent says to take the reciprocal and change the sign of the exponent, so $9^{-1/2} = 1/9^{1/2}$. A fractional exponent ½ says to take the square root, so $1/9^{1/2} = 1/\sqrt{9}$, which equals $1/3$.

9. Answer: c. Let x = the proportionality constant. 4x = $1,600,000, so x = $400,000. 6x + 4x + 2x = 12x, substitute x = $400,000, so 12 * $400,000 = $4,800,000. The players received 6 * $400,000 = $2,400,000, 4 * $400,000 = $1,600,000, and 2 * $400,000 = $800,000. Check: $2,400,000 + $1,600,000 + $800,000 = $4,800,000.

10. Answer: e. -5.1×10^{-2} by $3.9 \times 10^4 = (-5.1 * 3.9)$ $* (10^{-2} * 10^4) = -19.89 * 10^2 = (-19.89/10) * (10^2 * 10) = -1.989 \times 10^3$. Note that b is an equivalent answer, but it is not in scientific notation.

11. Answer: d. Let the number be x; $.125(x) = 48$, x $= 48/.125 = 384$

12. Answer: c. $600 = 100 * 6 = 10^2 * 6$, $\sqrt{600} = \sqrt{(10^2 * 6)} = \sqrt{(10^2)} * \sqrt{6} = 10\sqrt{6}$.
$150 = 25 * 6 = 5^2 * 6$, $\sqrt{150} = \sqrt{(5^2 * 6)} = \sqrt{(5^2)} * \sqrt{6} = 5\sqrt{6}$. $10\sqrt{6} - 5\sqrt{6} = 5\sqrt{6}$.

13. Answer: b. $\dfrac{x-y}{-z+w} = \dfrac{1--1}{-1-1} = \dfrac{2}{-2} = -1$

14. Answer: b. $1.234567 \times 10^5 \times 10^{-2} = 1.234567 \times 10^3 = 1234.567$; 3 is in the tenths place.

15. Answer: c. The y's are increasing by a constant positive amount, 2, which eliminates choices a, d, and e, even though those choices do work for x = 1 and y = 3. The constant positive amount is the slope. Only choice c has a slope of 2.

16. Answer: b. (4.67 hours/20 pounds) = (x hours/14 pounds). x = 4.67 * 14/20 = 3.269 hours. (.269 hours) * (60 minutes/1 hour) = 16.14 minutes, or 16 minutes rounded. Answer: 3 hours, 16 minutes. Do not use information from any other source such as your family tradition to answer this.

17. Answer: e. $(9x^2 + 8x - 6) - (2x^2 - 5x) - (-5x^3 - 3x^2 + 4) = (9x^2 + 8x - 6) + (-2x^2 + 5x) + (5x^3 + 3x^2 - 4) = (5x^3) + (9x^2 - 2x^2 + 3x^2) + (8x + 5x) + (-6 - 4) = 5x^3 + 10x^2 + 13x - 10$.

18. Answer: d. Use FOIL on $(x^3 + 2)(x^2 - 1)$:

    $x^3x^2 + x^3(-1) + 2x^2 + 2(-1) = x^5 - x^3 + 2x^2 - 2$.

    Note $x^3 x^2 = x^5$.

19. Answer: d. $F = (9/5)C + 32$. Subtract 32 from

    both sides to get $F - 32 = (9/5)C$. Multiply both

    sides by $(5/9)$ to get $(5/9) (F - 32) = C$.

20. Answer: d. Let x = Betty's age 5 years ago, $4x$ =

    Lou's age 5 years ago; 15 years from now,

    Betty will be $x + 20$, Lou will be $4x + 20$, and

    $4x + 20 = 2(x + 20)$. So, $4x + 20 = 2x + 40$,

    $2x = 20$, $x = 10$. Betty was 10 five years ago,

    Lou was 40 five years ago, and Lou is 45 now.

21. Answer: c. Let x = cost. Then $x + .225x = 490$.

    $1.225x = 490$, $x = 490/1.225 = 400$.

22. Answer: d. $(17 - 5)/(6 - x) = 3$; $12/(6 - x) = 3$;

    $12 = (6 - x)(3)$, $12 = 18 - 3x$, $-6 = -3x$, $x = 2$.

23. Answer: d. The slope m equals $(10 - 7)/(2 - 1) =$

    $3/1 = 3$. Use the equation $y - y_1 = m(x - x_1)$,

    with $x_1 = 1$ and $y_1 = 7$: $y-7 = 3(x - 1)$,

    $y - 7 = 3x - 3$, $y = 3x - 3 + 7$, $y = 3x + 4$. This is

    equivalent to $-3x + y = 4$, or $-6x + 2y = 8$.

24. Answer: a. The y-intercept b is 4 because the

    line includes the point $(0,4)$. Another point is

    $(8,0)$. The slope m equals $(0-4)/(8-0) = -.5$. In

    $y = mx + b$ format, the line is $y = -.5x + 4$.

25. Answer: d. Let the smallest number be x, the

    next be $x + 2$, and the largest be $x + 4$. Then

    $x + (x + 2) + (x + 4) = 171$; $3x + 6 = 171$,

    $3x = 165$, $x = 55$; $x + 2 = 57$; $x + 4 = 59$

26. Answer: d. Let u = unit's digit of original number, and 2u = ten's digit of original number. The original number = 10(2u) + u, which equals 21u. The reversed number is 10u + 2u, which equals 12u. We know that 21u = 12u + 27, so 9u = 27, u = 3. The original number is 63. Check: 63 = 36 + 27.

27. Answer: d. Let x = number of quarters, 2x = number of dimes, and 4x = number of nickels. Then .25x + .10(2x) + .05(4x) = 13; .25x + .20x + .20x = 13; .65x = 13; x = 13/.65 = 20; 2x = 40; 4x = 80. Answer: 40 dimes. Check: 20 * .25 + 40 * .10 + 80 * .05 = $13.00

28. Answer: c. The discounted price is 12 - 12 * .25

= 12 - 3 = 9. Let x = number of customers

paying $9, and 200 - x = number paying

$12.00. 9x + 12(200 - x) = 2250. 9x + 2400 -

12x = 2250. -3x = -150, x = 50. The

percentage paying $9.00 is 50/200 = 25%.

29. Answer: e. Let x = Harry's distance when they

meet, and 1.4 - x = Larry's distance.

Rate * Time = Distance, and they walk the

same amount of time. Harry's Time =

Distance/Rate = x/3, which equals Larry's Time

= (1.4 - x)/4; x/3 = (1.4 - x)/4; 4x = 3(1.4-x); 4x

= 4.2 - 3x; 7x = 4.2; x = 4.2/7; x = .6; 1.4-x=.8.

Answer: .6. Check: time = .6/3 = .2 = .8/4 = .5

30. Answer: c. Let x = quantity of 33% juice, and 20-x = quantity of 28% juice. Then .33x + .28(20-x) = .30 * 20. So .33x + 5.6 - .28x = 6, .05x = 0.4, x = .4/.05 = 8.

31. Answer: c. Let t = the time in hours to work together. Ann can do 1/3 of the job in 1 hour, or t/3 in t hours. Bob can do ½ of the job in 1 hour, or t/2 in t hours. Carol can do 1/4 of the job in 1 hour, or t/4 in t hours. If they work together they do the whole job, which equals 1. t/3 + t/2 + t/4 = 1. 4t/12 + 6t/12 + 3t/12 = 12/12, 13t = 12, t = 12/13.

32. Answer: a. Let x = amount invested at 6.5%, and x + $2,000 = amount invested at 8.0%. Then .065x + .08(x + $2,000) = 305. So .065x + .08x + 160 = 305, .145x = 145, x = $1,000

33. Answer: d. Let the sides, be x, x + 2, and x + 4.

The perimeter equals x + (x + 2) + (x + 4) =

3x + 6, which equals 2(x + 4) + 8 or 2x + 16.

So 3x + 6 = 2x + 16, x = 10, x + 4 = 14.

34. Answer: d. Angles x and 2x form a straight line,

so they are supplementary and add to 180.

2x + x=180; 3x = 180; x = 60, 2x = 120. Angles

2x and y are alternate interior angles and are

equal. Answer: 120°.

35. Answer: e. The triangles are similar.

$\triangle$ADE ~ $\triangle$ABC, so corresponding sides are

proportional. 18/24 = y/(y + 15); 18(y + 15) =

24y, 18y + 270 = 24y, 270 = 6y, y = 45.

36. Answer: b. Perimeter = 2(5x + 2) + 2(3x + 4) =

10x + 4 + 6x + 8 = 16x + 12 = 44, 16x = 32, x =

2. The base = 3x + 4 = 3 * 2 + 4 = 10.

Area = base *height, so height = area/base =

60 /10 = 6.

37. Answer: c. Circumference = π * diameter = 3.14 *

2 = 6.28. A 45° central angle is $^{45}/_{360}$ or $^{1}/_{8}$ of

the circle. The arc is ($^{1}/_{8}$) * 6.28 = .785

38. Answer: e. Volume of a cube = $(side)^3$, 125 =

$(side)^3$, so side = 5. The area of each face is

5^2 = 25, and there are six faces, so the surface

area = 6*25 = 150 square feet.

39. Answer: b. The volume of a prism equals (base area) * (height). The base is a right triangle with hypotenuse c = 5 and one leg b = 4, so by the Pythagorean Theorem a = $\sqrt{(5^2 - 4^2)}$ = 3. The area of the triangle is (1/2)(4)(3) = 6. V = (base area) * (height), so 60 = 6* height, and height = 10 feet.

40. Answer: c. Triangle III is a 180-degree rotation of Triangle I about the origin. Note that each original point (x,y) is transformed into the point (-x,-y).

41. Answer: c. Let r = radius of the smaller circle, and 2r = radius of the larger circle (because if the circumference of the larger circle is twice as large as the circumference of the smaller circle, then the radius of the larger circle is twice as large as the radius of the smaller circle). Area of smaller circle = πr^2, and area of larger circle = $\pi(2r)^2 = 4\pi r^2$. The area in between equals $4\pi r^2 - \pi r^2 = 3\pi r^2$. The ratio of the area in between the circles to the area of the smaller circle equals $3\pi r^2 : \pi r^2 = 3:1$.

42. Answer: d. Assume the box has length, width, and height of 1, so the radius of the can is ½. In two dimensions, area of circle is $\pi r^2 = \pi(1/2)^2 = \pi/4 = 3.14/4 = .785$, and area of square = 1 * 1 = 1. In three dimensions, both the circle and the square need to be multiplied by height of 1, which does not change the .785 and the 1. So, the can uses $^{.785}/_1 = 78.5\%$ of the box, leaving 21.5% unused.

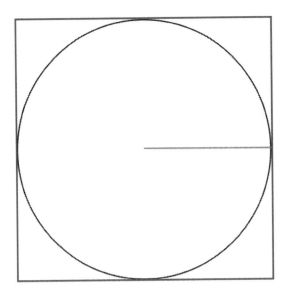

43. Answer: c. Volume of cone = $(1/3)(\pi)r^2h$. For

larger cone, $V = (1/3)(\pi)5^2 20 = (500/3)\pi$. For

smaller cone, $V = (1/3)(\pi)2^2 8 = (32/3)\pi$. Upper

portion volume = $(500/3)\pi - (32/3)\pi = (468/3)\pi$.

44. Answer: b. There are 51 cards, of which 13 are

diamonds and 12 are hearts. It is not possible

to choose a diamond and a heart.

$^{13}/_{51} + {}^{12}/_{51} - {}^{0}/_{51} = {}^{25}/_{51}$.

45. Answer: c. There are 30 + 15 = 45 people who

saw one or more movies, and 15 + 5 = 20 are

Easterners. The answer is $^{20}/_{45}$.

46. Answer: c. There are 3 * 3 = 9 ways to select

two cards: {(A,A),(A,K),(A,Q),(K,A),(K,K),(K,Q),

(Q,A),(Q,K),(Q,Q)}. Only four ways have no

ace: {(K,K),(K,Q),(Q,K),(Q,Q)}. The answer is

$^{4}/_{9}$.

47. Answer: b. Probability of success is 60%, so the probability of failing is 40% and this is P(0). If she is successful with probability 60%, then the probability of a second success is also 60% so the probability of first success and second success is 60% * 60% = 36% and this is P(2). The probability of first success and second failure is 60% * 40% = 24% and this is P(1).

48. Answer: a. Range = Maximum value - Minimum Value = 55 - 10 = 45. Median = 40. Answer: 45 - 40 = 5.

49. Answer: c. Mean = (0 * 20% + 1 * 25% + 2 * 25% + 3 * 20% + 4 * 10%) = 1.75. Median occurs when the cumulative probability is 50%, which occurs at 2. Mode is most probable and is tied between 1 and 2.

50. Answer: e. Choices a through d can be

calculated from a stem-and-leaf diagram.

51. Answer: d. Multiply the percentages by the total

of 300 to get the following numbers of fans:

45, 75, 90, 60, 30. All statements are correct,

except d, because Chipmunks are 30 greater

than Deer.

52. Answer: e. The standard deviation measures on

average how much the data is different from

the mean, and this difference will not change

due to every data value increasing by 4.

53. Answer: d. The other answer choices are false.

54. Answer: a. Calculate Income = Price * Number

of Rooms: At $100, $100 * 120 = $120,000.

At $200, $200 * 65 = $130,000. The difference

is $10,000.

55. Answer: c.

56. Answer: d. 275 + 85 = 360 votes were counted

out of 500, so 500 – 360 = 140 were not

counted. If Candidate B received 0, Candidate

D could have received 140.

ABOUT THE AUTHOR

Jerry Tuttle, FCAS, MA is an actuary (insurance mathematician) and is an online college math teacher. He earned a Bachelor of Arts in math from Queens College and a Master of Applied Math degree from the University of Virginia. He worked for a number of property-liability insurance companies as an actuary, while earning the insurance designations of Fellow of the Casualty Actuarial Society (FCAS), Chartered Property Casualty Underwriter (CPCU), and Associate in Reinsurance (ARe). He completed a Master of Arts in educational technology from New Jersey City University and has been an online college math teacher for several colleges for over 10 years. He actively tutors prospective teachers in person for the Praxis Core Math exam.

Jerry is a member of the National Council of Teachers of Mathematics and American Mathematical Association of Two Year Colleges and several of their state affiliates. He is a frequent speaker at these organizations, speaking on topics such as copyright in math teaching, cartoons in math class, order of operations, and computer simulation. He also speaks to local high schools and colleges about actuarial careers.

He has three sons, none of whom has inherited the math gene.

ABOUT THE BOOK

Do you want to become a teacher? Then you need to pass the Praxis® Core Math or a similar state exam. The Praxis Core Mathematics (5732) exam is given by the Educational Testing Service (ETS). This exam contains 56 short-answer questions that you take in a computer-delivered manner in 85 minutes. The author is a college-math teacher who tutors students for this exam.

This book contains sample problems the author uses in tutoring students for the exam. These problems are harder than you will find in other study guides, but the author hopes you will be better prepared with harder problems than easier ones. The book contains problems for each major topic, two full sample exams, and the exam's problem solutions.

18556134R00137

Made in the USA
Middletown, DE
01 December 2018